KEEP PRESSING ON

By Joel Iarmour

Introduction

It has been said that life is 10% what happens to you and 90% how you react to it. The trouble with the 10% is that it often catches us unprepared and throws us off balance leaving us struggling to steady ourselves again. I intend to outline here a rough guide to pressing on and in the process examine some underlying principles which it is hoped will help us to react better to that 10%.

In Yann Martel's prize winning novel 'Life of Pi' the adventure is told of a sixteen year old boy named Pi who after the tragic sinking of a cargo ship is left as the only human survivor on one solitary lifeboat bobbing on the wild, blue Pacific. For the entire journey of survival on this lifeboat Pi has the company of a 450 pound Royal Bengal Tiger. It is an outrageous scenario but one which the author uses to introduce a variety of plausible occurrences. The reader observes through the boy Pi the sheer audacity of the human spirit to survive against the tide of adverse circumstances. There are many setbacks for Pi as he tries to stay dry and warm, to find food, to quench thirst and to avoid provoking the Tiger. His survival techniques improve as he learns from each setback and tries to avoid repeating the same mistakes.

Life can throw up outrageous scenarios which may not involve spending time on the ocean with a Bengal Tiger but which we find no less intimidating. If you feel like you're being intimidated towards giving up by one challenge after another then our discussion here is aimed at encouraging you to keep pressing on and not 'throw in the towel'.

It serves us better to see challenges as teachers and we can learn much as we press through setback after setback without giving up. Former British Prime Minister Winston Churchill who led the nation through the darkest days of the Second World War declared:

Success is the ability to go from one failure to another, with no loss of enthusiasm.

We need to keep having a go at life knowing that we will likely stumble and fall along the way more often than not. This doesn't make us failures. That may only be said when we lose enthusiasm to keep trying.

What follows here is not an exhaustive solution to how we keep pressing on when we struggle to see the point of doing so. This author writes from the perspective of the Christian faith and this perspective maintains that God fills in the blanks where otherwise there is no clear direction for pressing on through the storms life throws at us. However, Christians should not 'throw the baby out with the bathwater' and need to take hold of certain principles relevant for all of us who need help to keep pressing on. Problems happen to Christians the same as anyone else; just because they put God into the equation doesn't mean they are somehow shielded from the realities of everyday circumstances. Unfortunately, the Christian message is sometimes presented as 'come to God and have all your needs met' which leads people to respond in the belief that as soon as they come to faith all their problems suddenly disappear. Then they find it difficult to keep going when the realisation dawns that becoming a Christian offers no immunity to the trials everyone else has to deal with. They also feel guilt if they're not constantly living in glorious victory over every obstacle that comes their way as they think a 'good' Christian should be. What they need to grasp is that whilst the God of the Bible is able to meet every need He doesn't beam up all the Christians and remove them from the experience of living in this world with all its stresses and strains. Everyone gets tested, Christians get tested. So, the themes we examine here are for both Christians and non Christians alike. Themes to be covered include:

- Slowing down and finding rest
- Learning there is an appointed time for breakthrough along with how we handle the waiting process
- Stepping from fear to faith and how we receive strength in our weakness
- Submission to processes which God allows us to go through
- Straightening up from what is keeping us bent over and hindering progress
- Examining our motivation
- Throwing off distractions and letting go of excuses
- Remembering why we left the past behind as we press on with no looking back
- Staying vigilant on the road ahead and through patient perseverance not allowing vision to die

Chapter 1

The Place of Rest

Slow Down

The roads we drive on have signs at various intervals warning of hazards ahead. Among them are plenty of 'slow' signs, for example when the motorist approaches a built up area or a bend in the road. Of course, some ignore the signs to slow down. This may be down to the impatient culture we live in or because people are rushing around with busy lives trying to get as many things done in a day as possible or they're conscious of an impending deadline. Whatever the reason(s) it is dangerous to ignore the slow signs. Nine times out of ten you might get away with it but it only takes one time for disaster to strike, resulting in serious injury or fatalities. I recall seeing TV ads with the message 'Slow Down, Speed Kills' which showed dramatic reconstructions of cars crashing at different speeds.

If we compare our lives to driving on a road, there are various points where we encounter signs to slow down. It's important to pay attention to them if we are to avoid an unnecessary collision. Our physical bodies send us messages like 'tired need rest', 'hungry, please feed me', 'thirsty need drink'. Friends and family send us slow down signs like 'you're not looking too well these days' or 'you haven't been yourself lately'. We can also become internally aware that we need to slow down. All these signs might as well not be there if we are determined to keep storming ahead without showing proper concern or awareness. Whilst there are occasions calling for greater speed (i.e. a motorway journey) speed becomes our enemy when we approach those blind bends in our lives and can't be sure of what's around the corner. When we slow down it gives us more breathing space to react whereas too much speed has the opposite effect. After more than twenty years of driving I've become increasingly aware of hazards on the road and so I keep my speed down more than I used to. The longer we travel on life's road the more aware we become of the potential for trouble ahead. Perhaps you've learned to slow down more than you used to. If not, then perhaps you need to pay greater heed to those slow signs and gain vital time to deal with whatever confronts you.

The unavoidable reality

No matter how much we try to avoid it, the truth is at some point we are going to become weary. We are not designed as robots or machines. We cannot keep going indefinitely without proper rest. Time slows for no one but we need to slow down and have a check up on a regular basis. Our body and soul needs routine maintenance. At the end of popular 1980s movie 'Ferris Bueller's Day Off', Ferris remarks "Life moves pretty fast, if you don't stop and look around once in a while, you could miss it!" The movie is about a high school senior who skips school on a nice spring day by faking illness to his parents.

My Father used to like saying "Time waits for no man". As a Father myself I realise only too well how it seems one minute your children are toddlers, the next they're driving cars. I'm not advocating skipping school (or work) to 'stop and smell the roses' but it's essential we slow down in our lives long enough to see what's happening. Life is not meant to be lived at a nonstop pace. A grand prix car still needs pit stops during a race. We need to pull in to those pit lanes along life's road circuit in order to receive necessary maintenance and advice.

When was your last check up?

Some people avoid visiting doctors. They would rather just soldier on with coughs and flu symptoms. Others feel they're too busy for time out to see a doctor or too worried about what the boss at work will say if the doctor signs them off for a while. This is ok at one level and I'm not suggesting we all act like hypochondriacs and rush to the doctor every time we develop a cough or common cold. However, it becomes a problem when we know something is wrong with us and it's not being improved through avoiding medical advice. Life inevitably brings its fair share of challenges which leave us weary and drained. We need a check up in our own lives now and again to assess the damage. It's not going to serve us well to leave it too long. When was your last check up and I'm not just talking medical but emotional and spiritual as well? Weariness is an unavoidable reality. We need time out to take stock and recharge. When I started my current job the employer required an official medical check up. It had been years since my last one. Thankfully everything checked out but it could've easily been different. I currently own a car which is over 3 years old and in the UK this means it legally requires an annual examination known as an MOT to determine its roadworthiness for another 12 months. Parts start falling off old cars that don't undergo MOTs and we start falling apart physically and emotionally if we don't stop and examine what is happening. If the grand prix car ignores pit stops it will likely breakdown with mechanical failure or spin off the track with worn tyres. If we ignore warning signs to slow down and rest we will either breakdown completely or spin off in a state of despair.

An Invitation to find rest

On social network sites like Facebook people who you have accepted as 'friends' can invite you to attend events. On my Facebook account I appreciate receiving such invites even if I can't attend them. Invitations don't always come at a convenient time but they do call for a response. The Christian message issues a particular invitation to a place of rest:

Come to me, all you who are weary and burdened, and I will give you rest. Take my yoke upon you and learn from me, for I am gentle and humble in heart, and you will find rest for your souls. For my yoke is easy and my burden is light (Matthew 11v28-30).

The Bible invites us to find rest in Jesus Christ. All of us look for meaning and purpose in this world and we can work away at doing many things to make it all 'seem' more meaningful. The Bible teaches that no amount of doing on our part will make up for what we lack without God at the centre of our lives.

It's an act of hospitality when someone invites you into their home. When God in Jesus Christ invites us to come and find rest for our souls it reveals His Heart of Hospitality towards all who accept it. The Biblical examples are plentiful of those who did accept it. We mentioned that some people avoid doctors. Well, Jesus didn't have that affect on people. The Jesus in the Bible is someone of immense quality who was a magnet drawing others toward him. People wanted to be where he was and to listen to his life changing words of life:

- ✓ *All the people hung on his words (Luke 19v48b)*
- ✓ *Because of his words many more became believers (Jn 4v41)*
- ✓ *Simon Peter answered him, Lord, to whom shall we go? You have the words of eternal life (Jn 6v68)*
- ✓ *Even as he spoke, many put their faith in him (Jn 8v30)*

Jesus makes a deep impact on people's lives. They want to come to him. They follow him, pursue him, invite him, and call out to him:

- Two disciples of John the Baptist asked Jesus where he was staying. He invited them to come and see. *So they went...and spent the day with him* (see Jn 1v35-9)
- Andrew brought his brother Simon (renamed Peter) to Jesus (Jn 1v41-2)
- Philip told Nathanial about Jesus and urged him, *come and see* (ref Jn 1v45-6)

We often carry baggage through life that we weren't made for and no amount of the 'carry on regardless' attitude will stop us growing weary at some point and needing rest. Footballers attend a lot of training sessions to keep fit for matches but after ninety minutes of play the legs do not want to keep going much longer. We need to acknowledge our weariness at some point. You've maybe come across the phrase 'only the fittest survive'. Well, for the Christian it is only those who rest in God and His love for us who survive:

He gives strength to the weary and increases the power of the weak. Even youths grow tired and weary, and young men stumble and fall; but those who hope in the Lord will renew their strength. They will soar on wings like eagles; they will run and not grow weary, they will walk and not be faint (Isaiah 40v31)

No amount of physical training, self-discipline or willpower can sustain us like God's rest. This rest centres on knowing that through Jesus nothing separates us from God's everlasting love.

Know your Limits

The actor Clint Eastwood quipped in one of his movies: 'a man's got to know his limitations'. This idea has relevance for all of us. There are limits to what we can do and to what we can endure. We cannot breathe properly at a certain altitude. We cannot survive at a certain depth under the sea. There are boundaries in our lives and the world we live in. Limits have been set despite today's mantra of 'maximise your potential' and 'you can do anything you put your mind to'. This is not being negative, it is just reality.

God does not operate within our limits. Jesus said that what is impossible for man does not apply to God:

> All things are possible with God (Mark 10v27)

To the early church Paul quoted from the Old Testament prophet Isaiah:

> No eye has seen, no ear has heard, no mind has conceived what God has prepared for those who love Him (1 Corinthians 2v9, cross ref Isaiah 64v4)

We need to find a place of rest as we become aware of our own limitations. If we arrive at a place of rest in God then there are no limits to what He can do within us.

Chapter 2

The Snare of Reasoning

One of the miracles of Jesus recorded in the Gospels involves him calming a storm. In Matthew's account it is stated that the storm came about *without warning* (Mt. 8v24). Jesus was asleep as the waves swept over the boat. The disciples woke him to point out that they were going to drown (V.25). Mark's version adds the disciple's remark, *Teacher, don't you care if we drown?* (Mark 4v38b).

Perhaps you're facing difficult circumstances that seemed to appear without warning. It seems as though God is ignoring your plight or is asleep on the job. You can either wait for God to calm the storm or, as you begin to question what is happening, attempt to reason out your own solution.

A church leader who I learned a lot from once urged me to avoid what he termed 'The Paralysis of Analysis'. Trying to understand God's ways before deciding to trust Him brings a kind of paralysis to the process of allowing His plans and purposes to unfold in our circumstances.

Watching a movie with my children can be an enjoyable leisure activity. Sometimes though in our house it has led to frustration. When my son hasn't understood the plot he asks questions as others are trying to concentrate on watching the movie. During these occasions it has been difficult to bring him from a position of confusion to one of clarity. I've had to actually press the pause button on the TV remote control several times to address my son's questions. The discussion usually ends with: "just watch the film and see what happens or we'll switch it off and forget the whole thing completely".

When we don't understand God's plot in our lives it may throw up lots of questions but if we try forcing answers it's like pressing the pause button on the process God is doing within us. The process becomes 'paralysed by analysis' and it would be better for God to switch it off completely and forget the whole thing. This can be avoided but it requires that we walk in unfamiliar territory:

Prov.3v5, *Trust in the Lord with all your heart and lean not on you own understanding.*

Let's consider the phrase *'all your heart'*.

When God prompted Samuel about whom to anoint as the next king of Israel to replace Saul, Samuel heard God's assertion:

Man looks at the outward appearance, but the Lord looks at the heart (1 Sam 16v7)

When King Saul's son Jonathan asked his armour bearer for his support to move towards the area where the Philistine enemies were hanging out the armour bearer replied:

Go ahead; I am with you heart and soul (1 Sam 14v7b)

An amplification of this statement might read: "go ahead my heart is with you, accomplish what you want in my life. I will not try to work it out before I commit my heart to the process". This means it's a done deal; no debate is necessary. It's not unlike what NASA would say during a countdown to launch: 'We are a go for lift off'. For God's purposes to have lift off He looks to see that our hearts are with Him.

At the time of writing I'm approaching my twentieth wedding anniversary. My wife had my heart before my head. I loved her before I understood everything about her. After nearly twenty years together we are still learning about each other. Love came before understanding.

As the nation of Israel was at the border of their Promised Land one of the reminders they are given over and over is:

Love the Lord your God with all your heart and with all your soul and with all your strength (Deuteronomy 6v5; 10v12; 11v13; 13v3; 30v6, v10)

Jesus repeats this when asked to identify the greatest commandment in the Written Law (see Matthew 22v37).

God doesn't ask us to love Him with all our reasoning, He asks simply that we love and trust Him with all our heart.

It's tempting to try reasoning out ways of tackling storms that envelop us, particularly if it looks as though God doesn't care that we appear to be drowning.

The bible makes it clear that God does care:

1 Pet. 5v7 *cast all your anxiety on him because he cares for you.*

Indeed, the apostle Paul prayed for the Church that its members would **grasp how wide and long and high and deep is the love of Christ (Eph. 3v18).**

The dilemma for many arises when God allows us to endure prolonged hardship. During such times, the voice of reasoning inside our heads can almost overwhelm us. The voice of reasoning within me has, in the past, identified two key questions:

Why, God, Why?

Scientists are constantly trying to answer the meaning of the Universe and we live in a world where human reasoning is not happy to live with unanswered questions.

A character in the Bible who was expected to live with unanswered questions was a man named Job. He is described as a man who pleased God. Yet, through no fault of his own, God allowed him to lose his wealth, family and even his health. Job's friends couldn't resist trying to reason out what was happening to him and told him he must have done something to cause the suffering. In fact, no reason is given and the so-called friends are admonished for their pride and arrogance in presuming to understand God (see Job 42v7-8).

When I picked up a sporting injury in my early twenties which left me in a wheelchair for a week and in crutches for two months afterwards, I would not have been very receptive if well-meaning 'comforters' had suggested I had done something to deserve my predicament. Sometimes hardship befalls us as a result of poor choices we make, but there are many instances when it is beyond our control or understanding.

For Job and for believers in Christ today, there is a requirement to press on through difficulty with unanswered questions in tow. True fellowship with the presence of God in this scenario is about being satisfied that God has a purpose even if we don't know what it is.

Jer. 29v11 begins, *for I know the plans I have for you, declares the Lord.*

Notice here that God is very clear about the plans He has for us and that is sufficient for Him. It needs to be sufficient for us.

When, God, When?

If you have given up asking the why question, you may still be wanting God to set a time limit on your suffering. This leads to another test:

> 1 Pet.5v10, *And the God of all grace, who called you to his eternal glory in Christ, after you have suffered <u>a little while</u>, will himself restore you and make you strong, firm and steadfast (emphasis added).*

How long is God's little while? No one knows and so we cannot pre-empt God's intervention because we have decided that it has been long enough coming. God has His own idea of a little while but He also promises to *restore* us and make us *strong, firm* and *steadfast.*

It is made clear that He *Himself* will do this – we don't have to manipulate Him into it. God knows we have limits to what we can bear (see 1 Cor. 10v13) and He will strengthen us we rely on Him.

Though we can't know the duration of God's little while, it won't help to throw a tantrum and cry 'why are we waiting'? This is what King Saul did when the prophet Samuel didn't fulfil an appointment with him at exactly the time Samuel himself had set. Saul couldn't get his head round this and so proceeds to act without Samuel. Just as he finishes this solo effort Samuel arrives and challenges him: *what have you done* before adding *you acted foolishly* (see 1 Sam 13v8-13). If Saul had just waited that little bit longer...but he didn't because his heart wasn't in it. He leaned on his own understanding and God knew He had to look elsewhere for a king with a different heart (v14).

There are times when I've had a question rolling around in my head: 'why am I waiting'? The lesson to take away from King Saul's example is: 'if I'd just waited a little longer'.

Waiting with the Right Attitude

Concerning this waiting game, it's not just necessary that we simply wait on God's timing. We might be doing this begrudgingly and with growing resentment towards God. So, it's important that our waiting is conducted in the right attitude. I do not always get this right, but one biblical example has helped guide me towards an 'improving' attitude:

Heb. 3v8-11, *do not harden your hearts as you did in the rebellion, during the time of testing in the desert, where your fathers tested and tried me and for forty years saw what I did. That is why I was angry with that generation, and I said, their hearts are always going astray and they have not known my ways. So, I declared on oath in my anger, they shall never enter my rest.*

God performed a vast array of miracles for the Old Testament Israelites under Egyptian slavery which eventually moved Pharaoh to release them (see Exodus 7-12) and then more miracles followed during their wilderness experience (Exodus 15 bitter water turned sweet; Exodus 16 Manna from heaven, to name but two). What positive effect did this have on them? Answer = none. They never stopped moaning. Put yourself in God's position. What's the point in Him providing miracles or answering pleas for help if every time He does the recipient finds something else to moan about? That's why it's so important to wait on God's timing with the right attitude and I'm glad this warning from Israel's history is in the Bible. God's warnings are not attempts to get heavy with us. On the contrary, they are actually signs of His grace, whereby He looks to save our lives from shipwreck and devastation.

When the famous ocean liner, Titanic, sank on its maiden voyage after hitting an iceberg, it came to light after the tragedy that numerous radio warnings about icebergs had been sent but, unfortunately, were not properly adhered to. Let us avoid 'The Titanic Syndrome' by not hardening our hearts as we wait on God's timing.

The Appointed Time

Before I was offered my current job, I had to wait more than two years after my application form was posted. It was five months before I even had a reply acknowledging that my application had been received. This informed me that it would be another eleven months before my assessment/interview process would begin. After passing every test required, administrative delays and changes to the admission process resulted in my not being offered a place for another eighteen months after this. The waiting process was very difficult for me as friends and family could testify, for they knew I was unhappy in the job I was doing at the time. The local church I belong to was praying for me and I learned something of waiting on God's timing. In having to wait on God's timing in different situations I've been impacted by a particular verse in the Bible:

Gal. 6v9 (New Living Translation), ***so don't get tired of doing what is good. Don't get discouraged and give up, for we will reap a harvest of blessing at the appropriate time.***

The New King James Version replaces the appropriate time with the phrase **in due season**. We live through various seasons of weather; autumn, winter, spring and summer. The plants and animals tell us very clearly when each season is upon us. The seasons arrive when they are due and not before. At the end of summer, farmers gather in the crops at harvest time. A harvest of spiritual blessing awaits us in due season if we do not give up. Take a step further in trusting God and not your own understanding. Be strong in God's empowering grace as you wait on His perfect timing. It has been said about God that He's never too early, He's never too late, He's always on time.

Chapter 3

What Are You Doing Here?

As strange as it may sound, many followers of Christ actually become quite comfortable and settled in their weariness. It becomes a cave of retreat, a cave which imprisons them. Here the walls go up, creating strongholds designed to stop the outside world hurting them again.

I retreated into such a cave after my parent's separation and made myself so comfortable that climbing out became very difficult.

I relate to the Old Testament character of Elijah who suffered great highs and lows. One moment he was on spiritual cloud nine after God worked through him to discredit the prophets of the false god, Baal (1 Kings 18). Shortly after this, he's hiding in a cave (1 Kings 19) and wallowing in self-pity, as evil queen Jezebel vows revenge. In this cave he hears the life transforming word of the Lord, ***What are you doing here, Elijah (19v9)?*** Notice it <u>doesn't</u> say, what are you doing <u>there</u>? In other words, God is right there alongside Elijah in the cave. Elijah is slow to respond to the encouragement and so God repeats the message in the form of a gentle whisper (19v12). If you're weary and burdened, God's Spirit does not come to pressurise you. He comes as a still, small voice to encourage and lift you up. God encouraged Elijah in the cave that there was more for him to do (19v15-16). He encourages us to think along the same lines.

Venturing into harsh weather

If I'm at home and the weather outside is cold, windy, or generally uninviting, I am tempted to stay inside, where it is warm and comfortable. If I do venture out on such days it usually means putting on extra layers of clothing which is more effort than a t-shirt and shorts on a hot sunny day. The message to 'keep pressing on' involves leaving the house, the cave or wherever we are hibernating in our spiritual comfort zone. We are challenged to step out and step forward by faith when the spiritual weather appears cold and uninviting.

The ship is not made for the harbour

Someone once remarked that Christians do not tell lies, they just sing them! Well, I remember singing some words that really got me thinking. The words made the point that boats are not made to stay safe in the harbour but are made for sea and storm. I knew that I was living the Christian life as if I was designed for the safety of the harbour. It was time to bend more to the wind of the Holy Spirit which blows us out of the harbour towards deeper water and stronger waves.

Moving from fear to faith

You may think you've done enough to survive the storms of life thus far. You may be saying to yourself that if you pushed out any further into deeper water you'll crumble under the pressure. I sympathise with this concern. However, it limits what God seeks to do in our lives.

A phrase I would hear growing up in church circles was, *God loves us as we are, but not enough to leave us there.* Pressing on through the Christian life is about moving forwards, not standing still. Herein lays the challenge of moving from a position of fear to a position of faith. Jesus said, **don't be afraid; just believe (Mk. 5v36).** This is spoken to the synagogue ruler, Jairus, whose daughter had died. Jesus wasn't being insensitive. He wasn't scolding Jairus for lack of faith. He was saying, it's ok to feel fear but don't let fear limit what God can do in this situation. When fear is felt (as it will be), get hold of God and cling to Him in faith. Scripture records that Jesus ministered God's healing touch and Jairus' daughter was raised (5v41-2).

In Genesis 32, we see that Jacob was fearful about meeting his brother Esau again years after they had fallen out bad style, when Esau had vowed to kill Jacob (see Gen. 27v41). God reveals Himself in the situation and it transpires that Jacob wrestles with God in the mindset; *I will not let you go unless you bless me* **(Gen. 32v26).** The end result is that, although Jacob was in the midst of struggle, he looked for the blessing and found it (v.28). With God's help he moved from fear to an experience of deepened faith. If you're struggling at the moment, hear the encouragement, *don't* *be afraid, only believe* and look for that blessing in the midst of the struggle.

Wavering Faith

Jesus said to his disciples, *If you have faith as small as small as a mustard seed, you can say to this mountain, move from here to there, and it will move. Nothing will be impossible for you* **(Mt. 17v20).** The context here relates to the healing of a boy experiencing seizures. The boy's father brought him to the disciples but the boy was not healed (17v16). The situation calls for mustard seed faith. Earlier in Matthew's gospel the mustard seed is described as *the smallest of all seeds, yet when it grows, it is the largest of garden plants and becomes a tree, so that the birds of the air come and perch in its branches* **(Mt. 13v32).**

The faith of the boy's father had probably taken a hit as a result of the disciples' failure to operate in mustard seed faith. Indeed, Mark's gospel records him making a frank admission to Jesus at the point of asking for help, *I do believe; help me overcome my unbelief* **(Mk. 9v24).** So he has faith, but it is mustard seed faith that is wavering. That's ok, because it's God who makes things grow as we bring him an offering of mustard seed faith.

Your faith may be wavering at present in the midst of weariness and you may be giving yourself a hard time, convinced you don't measure up to what God requires. All God requires is that you draw close to Him at your point of need, even with your wavering faith.

You will be amazed at what God does. He is in the habit of strengthening our faith and lifting us up.

Consider the episode when the apostle Peter began sinking in the water as he attempted to get to Jesus (see Mt. 14v28-30). Peter has come in for a lot of criticism on this one as we observe how he takes his gaze off Jesus and almost goes under when he becomes more concerned about the wind. However, we can draw out encouragement from this part of Peter's faith journey because despite his <u>wavering</u> faith Peter still manages to get out of the boat and does, for a while, walk on water. Even when he begins to sink, Jesus reaches out and catches him (Mt. 14v31).

If you're in the boat of difficult circumstances being tossed about by stormy waters, don't listen to the lie that the safest place is always in the boat. John Ortberg wrote a book entitled, *'**If you want to walk on water, you have to get out of the boat'.** How true this is. So, don't panic that you might begin to sink as you leave the comfort zone of staying tired and weary. Try reaching out to God with that basic offering of mustard seed faith. God will not let you drown.

Letting go of excuses

When God met with Moses in the Midian desert and tasked him to lead the Israelites out of Egyptian slavery, Moses threw up excuses: I'm no one special (Ex. 3v11); what shall I say (v13)? ; What if the Israelites don't believe me or listen to me (4v1)? ; I'm not good at speaking (4v10); he even suggested that God send someone else (4v13).

Moses had a choice to make: stay in the wilderness or take hold of God's more for him. **We have to decide if we want God's more for us**. We can choose to take it or leave it.

In the previous chapter, I referred to leaving a job I didn't enjoy. Prior to my leaving, I made a choice to respond to the sense I had that God wanted more for me. For a while, I battled with excuses to stay where I was: I'm not qualified to do anything else; what if the next job isn't any better? Sound familiar? I now have a better appreciation that the process of stepping further into God's purpose for my life involves the choice to decide what I want and let go of excuses holding me back.

Jesus once encountered a man who had been disabled for 38yrs (see Jn. 5v1ff.). Jesus asked him, *do you want to get well (v6)?* The man's response was a laboured excuse blaming others for holding him back and going on about how he needed someone to help him (v.7). Jesus confronted the issue of excuses head on by telling the man to *get up* (v8). In other words, **the road to his healing began with his own response not those of other people**. Again, Jesus is not being insensitive. In fact, he recognises this disadvantaged person needs a helping hand and is available to meet that need. The man's situation changes dramatically as he lets go of excuses and does what Jesus tells him. If we need breakthrough in our lives, help is at hand. A verse of scripture which points us in the right direction is **Ps. 46v1, *God is our refuge and strength, an ever-present help in trouble.*** Perhaps you need to be still before the Lord and allow these truths to stir you into action. So, get up, step forward, leave the cave, move out of the harbour, and get out of the boat. It's time to respond to the voice of the Holy Spirit asking, *what are you doing here?*

Chapter 4

The Sufficiency of God's Grace

The grace of God is such a vast subject that it cannot be summarized in the space allotted here. Yet, whenever I try to fathom God's lavish grace or rely on the sufficiency of it, I consider

Jn 3v16, *For God so loved the world that He gave His only begotten Son, that whoever believes in Him should not perish but have everlasting life (NKJV).*

God's grace is often described as 'getting what we don't deserve', or put simply, 'His Unmerited Favour' to a world pursuing its own desires. For me it goes far beyond this. As I seek now to make every day a 'cross centred day', I am conscious that my life cannot be built on what I do but on what God, by grace, has done for me already. He sent Jesus to die on a cross for all our wrongdoings – a debt we can never repay. This act of grace pours over my life with increasing measure and empowers me to keep pressing on.

During my school years I was quite a talented sportsman and was selected for school teams in no less than five different sports. My biggest problem was, however, that I lacked the confidence or self-belief to be the best that I could be in these activities. I look back at this period of my life with the benefit of hindsight and see that I put a tremendous amount of pressure on myself to earn acceptance from others through my sporting performances. I stayed in a performance driven mindset for a long time. I did not have revelation that I could be free in God's grace and that, in His eyes, my success is not based on personal performance.

Eph. 2v8-9...*it is by grace you have been saved, through faith – and this not from yourselves, it is the gift of God – not by works, so that no one can boast.*

When I opened my life to receive God's grace in Jesus Christ, I did not automatically feel a very confident person and my previous tendency to perform my way to acceptance from others carried through to the Christian life. I am still progressing in this area and have not 'arrived' yet. I am more aware now that God, in Christ, loves me unconditionally.

Rom. 8v31-2 *What, then, shall we say in response to this? If God is for us, who can be against us?*

Some days you may feel as though no one is for you. Perhaps you feel put down at work or misunderstood by those around you. Your reaction to these scenarios determines whether or not you live in slavery or freedom.

Gal 5v1 *It is for freedom that Christ has set us free. Stand firm, then, and do not let yourselves be burdened again by a yoke of slavery.*

In Christ, God has set us free - we are accepted and forgiven. We still have responsibility to do what is right, but our acceptance before God is based not on what we do or how others view us. The bible reveals that, by faith in Christ and all he accomplished on the cross, Christ's righteousness is imparted to us and we are given a position of right standing before God. This is called justification (see Rom 3v21-6). I encourage you as you read these words to cling to the God of grace and know the truth of who you are in Christ.

Jn. 8v31-2, *if you hold to my teaching you are really my disciples. Then you will know the truth and the truth will set you free.*

Jn 8v36, *if the son sets you free, you will be free indeed.*

Jesus called the devil, 'Father of Lies' (Jn.8v44) and through his lies he wants to rob Christians of living free in God's grace by giving them a false notion of themselves.

Ok, so you may not be eloquent

When God decided to use Moses as His instrument of rescuing Israel from Egyptian slavery, the response of Moses was uninspiring to say the least. One of the excuses he threw up revealed how inadequate he felt:

O Lord, I have never been eloquent, neither in the past nor since you have spoken to your servant. I am slow of speech and tongue (Ex. 4v10).

God, you've got it wrong

The angel of the Lord visited Gideon after Israel cried out for help against Midian. Gideon was addressed as 'Mighty Warrior' (Judges 6v12). Gideon seemed to think God was confused. He responded, *who am I to save Israel? My clan is the weakest in Manasseh, and I am the least in my family (Judges 6v15).*

These are just two examples of people who were overwhelmed with a sense of weakness, fear and inadequacy, yet through God's empowering grace went on to confound such unpromising beginnings. Take note, this is the way God still works among His people today:

Paul wrote to the Church at Corinth, *Think of what you were when you were called. Not many of you were wise by human standards; not many were influential; not many were of noble birth. But God chose the foolish...to shame the wise...the weak...to shame the strong...so that no-one may boast before Him (I Cor. 1v26-29 abbreviated).*

God isn't looking for self-sufficient people who believe they have it all together. He's looking for those who rely on the sufficiency of His grace and He uses various circumstances to prompt this reliance.

The Thorn in the Flesh

It is natural for us to rely on someone or something other than ourselves when our own resources are not enough. This is the ideal place for God's grace to intervene. We must take the first step to receive God's grace by acknowledging that we are not doing so well on our own and that we need His help. Often, God uses a mechanism to bring this about. In his writings to the church at Corinth Paul shares much about his personal hardships and none more so than 2 Cor.12v7, where he mentions a 'Thorn in the Flesh'. This is something God uses to keep Paul reliant on His empowering grace. We are not told what it is, but more importantly, God allowed it to last a significant length of time and it caused Paul a lot of suffering. Indeed, the word *torment* is used. Paul pleaded with the Lord to remove it on three separate occasions (2 Cor. 12v8). God's response is one of those standout moments in scripture, ***My grace is sufficient for you (2 Cor. 12v9).***

When I found myself in an unhappy working environment (referred to in chapter 2), this became a thorn in the flesh and the phrase, *My grace is sufficient for you* came to the fore once again.

Strength in weakness

The statement about God's grace being sufficient is unpacked with the explanation that His power is made perfect in human weakness (2 Cor. 12v9 b). It is not that God delights in our weakness so that he can make Himself look good. Rather, He determined that it is healthy for us to be kept aware that we need help and uses different situations to bring this about.

At the outset of 2 Corinthians it is recorded that Paul and his companions had known pressures far beyond their own ability to endure – so much so that they despaired even of life itself (2 Cor. 1v8). He goes on to elaborate that all this happened to deepen reliance on God, not themselves (v.9). God leads us to rely on Him in our weakness. This goes deeper than occasionally pressing the panic button. In full awareness of our human frailties we must cling to the *God of all grace* as if every move depended on it.

I live in a very scenic part of England near the Lake District. I'm in close proximity to some of the popular Lakeland Fells. When I scaled the one named Blencathra, I used the so-called 'Sharp Edge' route (sounds great doesn't it). Up to the point of reaching this Sharp Edge, I told myself it would not be a problem, but as I began to negotiate this section of the climb, I suddenly became very unsure of myself. Those old issues of lacking confidence and self-belief came to the fore again. On this occasion I'm glad to say I overcame the negative thoughts by first of all clinging closely to the rocks every step of the way and, secondly, by following the footsteps of my friend who guided me successfully along Sharp Edge and up to the Blencathra summit.

The Psalmist declares to God: *My soul clings to you; your right hand upholds me (Ps.63v8).* As the climber clings to the mountain we must cling to God who, by His grace, upholds us in the midst of our weakness. This may involve throwing off extra baggage that is surplus to requirements. When I scaled Blencathra, I filled my back pack with stuff I didn't need – it was too warm for the extra layers of upper body clothing I brought along. If anything, I had to remove a layer of clothing that was hampering my efforts. Our efforts to cling to God will be hampered if we carry aspects of self-sufficiency which are not required.

Each of my four children have known a stage of their growing up where they cling closely to the parents and look for constant attention from them (our youngest is still there). It is a challenge for parents. However, the 'clingy' stage is an opportunity to draw close to the children and spend quality time with them in various activities.

Our Father in Heaven seeks quality time with us and has immeasurable grace to lavish upon His children who cling to Him wholeheartedly. If we cling to God from the depths of our innermost being and draw on the richness of His wonderful grace, we discover that this grace is indeed sufficient for us in all circumstances.

Chapter 5

The God who sees us

In chapter 3 it was said that Peter in his wavering faith took his gaze off Jesus and began to sink. One of the truths about God which is good to focus on is that He never takes His gaze off us.

Psalm 121 is a beautiful reminder of this: it makes statements about God like, *He who watches over you will not slumber* **(v.3)**; *The Lord will keep you from harm – He will watch over your life* **(v.7)**; *the Lord will watch over your coming and going both now and for evermore* **(v.8).** So, we can receive encouragement to keep pressing on through hardship from the One who sees us and never stops watching and guarding over our coming and going.

What about Diversions?

Recently, my wife and I bumped into a friend in the centre of the town where we live. This friend was a mother who had her youngest child, a little boy, walking with her. Seconds after we began chatting, the boy had an accident whilst his mum's attention was momentarily drawn away from watching her son. Mum felt awful and my wife and I felt guilty for keeping her talking. Although, as I think back now the boy was doing something dangerous and if he had checked with his mum beforehand to see if it what he was doing was ok, he would've been guided away from harm.

Looking to God in all circumstances guides us way from harm and we can be assured that nothing will momentarily distract his attention from us. This doesn't mean we escape the bumps and bruises of various trials but God's eyes remain on us throughout.

In one of the last scenes from the movie version of Lord of The Rings, Frodo approaches the realm of the evil Sauron in an effort to finally destroy the ring which Sauron needs to destroy all opposed to him. At first the eye of Sauron appears to be watching everything and there is no way to escape his gaze. Then suddenly his eye turns away. This happens because the so-called armies of men march at Sauron's stronghold as a diversionary tactic – a tactic which works. Sauron's eye could not be everywhere at the same time and his attention could be drawn to something which he saw as a threat to his position.

God sees everything all the time. Furthermore, He is totally secure in who He is and His gaze will not turn to something which concerns Him more than what is happening to you. He cannot feel threatened because there is no name higher than His in all the earth.

Ps. 24v1 ***The earth is the Lord's and everything in it, the world and all who live in it.***

Ps. 47v2 ***How awesome is the Lord Most High, the great King over all the earth!***

God sees all situations everyone goes through and if we keep looking to Him even when the going gets tough we can be assured that His gaze remains on us at all times.

Ps. 33v13-14 *From heaven the Lord looks down and sees all mankind; from His dwelling-place He watches over all who live on earth.*

At this point you may be thinking, "well I've not listened to God and ended up in a mess, I've missed my chance, God won't be interested now". The good news is that nothing you've been through has escaped God's attention and because of this the situation can be rescued.

The example of Hagar

In Genesis Chapter 16, we read about a woman named Hagar who was mistreated by Abraham's wife Sarah. This arose from jealousy that Hagar was pregnant with Abraham's child and Sarah was barren. It got to the point where Hagar couldn't take any more abuse and ran away to the desert. God saw all this and spoke to Hagar in the desert, telling her to go back and submit to her mistress Sarah. He added that blessing would come as she submitted to this process (see ch.16: vv.6-10). In the midst of a difficult situation Hagar experienced fresh revelation to her about the nature of God. She recognised and acknowledged that God sees her:

Gen. 16v13 *She gave this name to the Lord who spoke to her: "You are the God who sees me," for she said, "I have now seen the One who sees me".*

Submit to the process

The example of Hagar and her desert experience shows us that the One who sees us may require that we go through a process to arrive at the point of seeing the One who sees us. Trusting God does not spare us from that desert experience (whatever it may be), especially if it's part of a process that leads to greater spiritual maturity, blessing and revelation about the nature of God Himself.

Hagar ran away when the going got tough but the God who sees us told her to go back and submit to a process. God understands our temptation to bail out when we are mistreated or finding circumstances difficult. When He requires us to go back and face what we fled He promises to be with us and help us.

Ps. 46v1 *God is our refuge and strength, an ever-present help in trouble.*

Joshua 1v9 *...Be strong and courageous. Do not be terrified; do not be discouraged, for the Lord your God will be with you wherever you go.*

Hagar is not alone in Biblical examples of those God told to go back to a place where they had fled from. Moses fled from Egypt to the desert of Midian and God sent him back. Elijah fled to the desert and the God who was with him in the desert cave, watching him, sent him back the way he came (see 1 Kings 19). Jonah ran away from a challenging task at Ninevah but once again the God who sees us sent him back.

Going back to mistreatment

Perhaps like Hagar you have been going through a period of mistreatment. It may be from a boss at work, other work colleagues, someone close to you, a friend, family member or partner. This can be incredibly hard to deal with. It may seem easier and justified to run away than to submit to a process which involves going back for more mistreatment. Perhaps you've already tried confronting this mistreatment and it hasn't worked; either the person doesn't recognise their behaviour is wrong or they are unwilling to behave differently. Have you considered that perhaps the only way forwards is backwards? What do I mean? I mean that moving away from an issue ignores it for a while but doesn't actually deal with it, whereas going back to it and working through it with God works much better. Then we can know forward momentum again as we travel backwards along the road we have just travelled.

Of course we can become very angry at being mistreated. But this anger is not dealt with properly by running away. When we run away in this state our anger runs away with us. I once read an interview from someone under the media spotlight who had been through a strained break up from his wife. He likened harbouring anger to drinking poison and expecting someone else to die. This is a good description of how anger can affect us. The God who sees us doesn't want us to drink this poison. Harbouring anger at being mistreated harms ourselves more than the other person and the Devil is the only one who wins in this scenario.

2 Corinthians 2v10-11 ...*what I have forgiven-if there was anything to forgive-I have forgiven in the sight of Christ for*

your sake, in order that Satan might not outwit us. For we are not unaware of his schemes.

Ephesians 4v26-27 *In your anger do not sin: Do not let the sun go down while you are still angry, and do not give the devil a foothold.*

I once tried to stay away from a particular town where I'd had a negative church experience. I definitely harboured anger as I did this. I went to a fellowship in another town 15 miles away. I was told almost as soon as I walked in the door that this group of believers intended to plant a church in the town I had run away from. God must have a sense of humour. I am now part of that church plant. It's been part of a process that God required me to submit to. It's not been an easy process and I resisted at first. However, I am now fully submitted to this process of moving forward by going back along the road I came. I can now say with an accepting smile, like Hagar, I see the One who sees me.

If God is speaking to you about going back the way you came in ways hinted at here, it will likely involve at least three things: letting go of anger; praying blessing for those who have mistreated you (see Luke 6v28); praying God's will to be done (see Luke 6v10 The Lord's Prayer). The end result may involve moving away from the influence of a person who has been mistreating you or God moving them on. But by then, if we have submitted to the process as a God thing, we arrive at a place of greater spiritual maturity and with hearts and minds at peace. With fresh revelation, having seen the One who sees us let us keep in mind the words of Peter:

For it is commendable if a man bears up under the pain of unjust suffering because he is conscious of God (1 Peter 2v19).

The Divine Lookout

On the night the Titanic liner sank during its maiden voyage in 1912 after it hit an iceberg, there was a crew member stationed at the lookout post. Usually the designated person had access to a set of binoculars. I watched a well researched TV documentary about what happened on the night in question which suggested the lookout did not have the necessary binoculars. Had they been used the fatal iceberg might have been spotted by the lookout sooner and tragedy averted. Aside from this the Titanic was supposedly sent a number of radio warnings about icebergs which either were not passed on or not taken seriously enough.

The God who sees us is like a Divine Lookout who sees the icebergs we may heading for in our lives or which may be heading towards us. He is on the lookout post by day and night:

Psalm 121v5-6 *The Lord watches over you- the Lord is your shade at your right hand; the sun will not harm you by day, nor the moon by night.*

He will not be caught asleep on the job and has no need of binoculars as His gaze sees what is ahead well before it reaches us:

Psalm 139v16*...All the days ordained for me were written in your book before one of them came to be.*

Any 'icebergs' on the horizon are warned about by our Divine Lookout who shouts a warning 'icebergs ahead' and these warnings help save our lives from shipwreck and devastation. Put your trust in the 'Lookout' who is best positioned to advise us in the direction we need to be steering. Be open to a fresh encounter with God where we are guided safely by the One who sees us.

Chapter 6

The Sacrifice of Praise

In 2 Chronicles 20 we learn about a vast army marching against the people of Judah, Israel's southern kingdom. After the initial shock, then encouragement to the people from King Jehoshaphat, followed by more reassurance from the priest Jahaziel about how God would help, we read:

2 Chron. 20v19 **Then some Levites** (priests) **from the Kohathites and Korahites stood up and praised the Lord, the God of Israel with a very loud voice.**

Also, **v.21** ..**Jehoshaphat appointed men to sing to the Lord and praise him for the splendour of his holiness as they went out at the head of the army, saying:**

"Give thanks to the Lord, for his love endures forever".

It's understandable to feel shock and alarm when a vast army of circumstances threaten to overwhelm us and our spiritual enemy, the Devil, looks as if he's trying to annihilate us. This is exactly how those in Judah felt when the armies of two other nations, Moab and Ammon, massed against them - 2 Chron. 20v3 uses the word *Alarm* to describe Jehoshaphat's initial reaction. Keeping that in mind, it's all the more remarkable to see how the King and people of Judah were able to offer up a sacrifice of praise to God. This truly was a sacrifice because it cost them – it wasn't easy to put aside all that fear and discouragement they would be feeling as a vast army approached intent on their destruction. Indeed, the devil tries to persuade us not to praise God.

The numbers game

It is said that the mind can play funny tricks with us. Certainly, our mind can start imagining all sorts of negative scenarios at mounting obstacles we see before us. In the Christian life, we are encouraged to *live by faith, not by sight* (2 Corinthians 5v7). We need to see with the eyes of faith (in God), not eyes focused on how the odds appear stacked against us.

Among the many property programmes which appeared on TV in recent years some have followed huge undertakings of either property restorations or dream homes built from scratch. At the outset of these ventures and even well into them the viewer sees all the rubble and mess and financial outlay and is led to think this looks hopeless. However, at some point these programmes usually include a tour of the glorious looking end result suggesting all the hard work was worthwhile. The success can be put down in large measure to those who were sure from the start about what they hoped for and totally determined to see it through despite the number of obstacles stacked against them.

Heb. 11v1, *Now Faith is being sure of what we hope for and certain of what we do not see.*

The message here is to change our focus if it is fixed on rubble, mess and drain on our resources. We need to keep the certainty of what God can do at the forefront of our minds and keep looking forward with eyes of faith, not do a runner when the going gets tough. Others before us wrestled with this. We've already pointed to Jehoshaphat's situation and there are various biblical examples:

- **Exodus 14** The Israelites were terrified as they saw the Egyptian army marching after them (see Ex. 14v10).
- **Numbers 13** Most of the Israelite scouting party to the land of Canaan took one look at the enemy and threw up a list of negatives like *the people who live there are powerful and the cities are fortified and very large* (v.28).
- **Judges 7** Israel felt outnumbered by the combined might of the Midianites, Amalakites and all other Eastern peoples, who, it says, had *settled in the valley, thick as locusts* (Judges 7v12). When Israel's leader Gideon first asked who wanted to leave the fight, 20,000 men did a runner.
- **2 Kings 18v17**, *The king of Assyria sent...a large army...to king Hezekiah at Jerusalem.* Hezekiah's initial response is that it's *a day of distress and rebuke and disgrace* (2 Kings 19v3).

Rather than being overwhelmed by the numbers that our spiritual enemy tries to throw at us we must draw on our faith in God and remember certain truths in order to move towards a sacrifice of praise.

God doesn't like to be insulted

When the ungodly King Ahab of Israel had to deal with the entire Aramean army coming to attack Samaria (Israel's then capital) it is apparent that God responds to the Aramaen's underestimation of Him:

> 1 Kings 20v28 ***The man of God came up and told the King of Israel, "This is what the Lord says: 'Because the Arameans think the Lord is a god of the hills and not a god of the valleys, I will deliver this vast army into your hands, and you will know that I am the Lord.***

Notice God's response had nothing to do with honouring a faithful King Ahab and his leading of Israel, in fact the Bible records that Ahab *did more evil in the eyes of the Lord than any of those before him* (see I Kings 16v30f.)

Let's be clear: God has a reputation to uphold and has purposed to fill the earth with His glory – a mission that was not lost on the psalmists:

> Ps. 57v5 ***Be exalted, O God, above the heavens; let your glory be over all the earth.***

> Ps. 72v19 ***Praise be to his glorious name for ever; may the whole earth be filled with his glory.***

This could be a starting place for us to sacrificially praise God in the midst of difficulty; lifting up the Name of God and walking in the truth that He will honour His Name, particularly if it is going to diminish in the eyes of others who may be thinking: 'Where is your God in all of this?'

So God is zealous for His Name and comes against those who trounce it:

- The shepherd boy David was aware that God's name is to be revered when he came against the insults of Goliath: *I come against you in the name of the Lord Almighty, the God of the armies of Israel, whom you have defied* (1 Samuel 17v45)
- King Hezekiah also believed God would act as Sennacherib insulted Him. As Sennacherib and his all conquering Assyrian army came near Jerusalem his message to Hezekiah was *How then can the Lord deliver Jerusalem from my hand?* (2 Kings 18v35). Hezekiah's prayerful response urged God to respond to these insults: *Give ear, O Lord, and hear; open your eyes. O Lord, and see; listen to the words Sennacherib has sent to insult the living God* (2 Kings 19v16).

It does not go unnoticed when people insult the Living God. Offer a sacrifice of praise to the One who will make His glory known whatever insults are thrown at His Name.

God will fight for you

Perhaps my best sporting achievement at school was when I batted all afternoon for the school cricket team and the opposition were not able to bowl me out. That innings was the highest for anyone in the school team that year and I was presented with an award for this during the final school assembly of the term. When I went into bat on that occasion the team needed a good innings from me to increase the chance of victory. So I was not just going in to bat to do myself proud, I was going into bat for the team and help them be victorious.

God goes into bat for those who put their trust in Him when difficult circumstances arise. He does it as has been stated to bring honour to His Name but also because He is on our team, He's on the same side and wants us to be victorious in battles we face. God recognises battles which are His to fight and we don't need to try fighting these for Him.

2 Chronicles 20v15...*'Do not be afraid or discouraged because of this vast army. For the battle is not yours, but God's*

- **1 Samuel 17v47** shows David's attitude on this as he moves to the battle line to face Goliath; *for the battle is the Lord's, and he will give all of you into our hands.*
- **Exodus 14v14** includes the phrase from Moses; *the Lord will fight for you.* As that situation progressed even the Egyptians pursuing Moses and the Israelites knew what was happening, *"Let's get away from the Israelites! The Lord is fighting for them against Egypt"* (v.25).
- **Joshua 6v16** when Joshua trusted God to fight the battle for Jericho, *Joshua commanded the people, "Shout! For the Lord has given you this city!*

- **Joshua 8v7** at the outset of the second attempt to take the city of Ai Joshua declares, *"you are to rise up from ambush and take the city. The Lord your God will give it into your hand".*

The Biblical evidence is clear, the case overwhelming – God promises to fight for you. The battle is His, not yours and this is yet another reason to offer the sacrifice of praise.

Get perspective

As part of my last job I used to visit a motorway service station that overlooked a picturesque lake area. At the viewpoint for visitors there was a plaque with a scripture verse inscribed on it. It was one of those scriptures that focused on the bigness of God and His role as Creator. During the busyness and hassles of the job reading that verse over the lake helped me to pause, reflect and get perspective again that God was in control and nothing was too difficult for Him. We all need those 'get perspective moments' and like the psalmist need to set aside time to be still and know that He is God (Ps.46v10).

2 Chron. 20v6-7 outline Jehoshaphat's perspective as a vast army comes against God's people:

"O Lord, God of our fathers, are you not the God who is in heaven? You rule over all the Kingdoms of the nations. Power and might are in your hand, and no-one can withstand you. O our God, did you not drive out the

inhabitants of this land before your people Israel and give it
forever to the descendants of Abraham your friend?

Before God fights for us there is often a time delay – an ideal
opportunity for us to get perspective. On a continual basis we need
to pause and keep enlarging our vision of a big God as
Jehoshaphat did. His statement highlights several aspects of God:

- o God is in heaven – He's not contained by our limitations
- o He rules over all – so He's sovereign and in control
- o Power and might are in His hand – it's all about what He can
     do not what we can do
- o No one can withstand Him – no obstacle too great for Him
- o He has done great things in the past to fulfil His promises to
     His people – it's good to reflect on God's past deeds and
     receive encouragement from previously answered prayer.

By getting hold of the 'Jehoshaphat perspective' and similar pictures
of the greatness of our God we can begin to offer that sacrifice of
praise.

Assume the Praise Position

> 2 Chron. 20v22 *As they began to sing and praise, the Lord*
> *set ambushes against the men of Ammon and Moab and*
> *Mount Seir who were invading Judah, and they were*
> *defeated.*

Notice that God made His move as Israel burst into praise at the
front of the army marching to meet the enemy. God's people had

assumed 'the praise position' and God loves to step in at this point and fight the battle which belongs to Him in an atmosphere of being praised for who He is. Jehoshaphat actually appointed people to position themselves for praise at the head of the army – a key part of his 'military' strategy was to have people in the praise position.

Recently, I injured my back. Through my job, I was able to access a physiotherapist. He gave me a list of exercises to aid my recovery and drew pictures of the positions I had to assume. Before I complete these exercises my body has to first be in the right position. Before we walk through the battles we face daily, God's Spirit prompts us to assume the right position – the praise position. When Paul and Silas were in prison for spreading the good news about Jesus, the Son of God, they began to lift up God's Name with singing. It was then that God stepped in and the prison doors broke open (see Acts 16). If we feel imprisoned by what's going on around us at the moment and God's intervention seems delayed it may be that He's giving you every opportunity to assume the praise position.

Talk to your soul

I'm often drawn to read Psalm 42. Here the psalmist tackles his 'down in the dumps' attitude and starts talking sense to his soul: *Why are you downcast, O my soul? Put your hope in God, for I will yet praise Him, my saviour and my God* **(Ps. 42v11).** So it's Biblical to chat with ourselves and give our souls a real talking to. Christians can remind themselves daily that in Jesus Christ they are made right with God and begin to praise Him:

Heb 13v15 *Through Jesus, therefore, let us continually offer to God a sacrifice of praise – the fruit of lips that confess his name.*

I have just watched the England football team play not very well in the first half of an important game. The commentators were speculating what the England manager would say to the squad during the half-time team talk in the changing room. The general consensus was that he would give them a real talking to and encourage them to play the second-half more confidently and stop looking like a team that was 'down in the dumps'.

Perhaps it seems like your life in God so far has not been going as expected. You may be looking, feeling and behaving like someone who is down in the dumps. Well it's time to give your soul that half-time talk. Although our eternal salvation is totally dependent on God's grace revealed in Jesus Christ, we still need to manage the attitude of our souls on a regular basis and it is good for us 'managers' to remind our souls that we should be living daily in the reality of what Christ accomplished for us in his death and resurrection. When was the last time you spoke to your soul and encouraged yourself in the Lord? Whatever you're going through it's never too late to talk to your soul with the challenge not to be so downcast and determine to start praising God again.

An assembly of praise

It's ok praising God on your own but there is something to be gained from meeting with other believers gathering to praise God. This is what's known as corporate praise. In **2 Chronicles 20** the way the nation of Judah praised God illustrates that corporate praise can be initiated in various ways:

- Spontaneous praise. As the people of Judah were face down in worship, the priests suddenly **stood up and praised the Lord...with a very loud voice (v.19).** I've been really blessed when gathered with other believers where there is a sudden burst of spontaneous (and loud) praise. There is something very uplifting about this and it's not something that is rehearsed or the result of people being told to do it. We must allow space in our church meetings for spontaneous bursts of praise.

- Appointed praise. **V.21 *Jehoshaphat appointed men to sing to the Lord and to praise Him for the splendour of His holiness as they went out at the head of the army..*** Church gatherings should begin with some form of praise and we often need people appointed to help us in this. It may be someone reading a passage of scripture or leading the church in prayerful praise or handing over to a worship group at the front of our gathering to lead us in bringing praise to God.

- Cause for Praise. **Vv.26-27** (After God had delivered Judah from Moab and Ammon) **the people assembled in the Valley of Beracah** (which means Valley of Praise), **where they praised the Lord.. Then, led by**

Jehoshaphat, all the men of Judah and Jerusalem returned joyfully to Jerusalem, for the Lord had given them cause to rejoice over their enemies.

God has given us cause to gather regularly with others and praise Him. It's a good thing to praise Him together when prayers are answered. I am always encouraged to hear testimonies of God's goodness when I meet with other Christians and this gives me further incentive to assemble for praise. We see the early church praise God when there is cause for it: **Acts 21v19-20** *Paul ..reported in detail what God had done among the Gentiles through his ministry. When they heard this, they praised God.*

I want to keep meeting with other Christians who are a praising people like the early believers: **Acts 2v46b-7...***They broke bread in their homes and ate together with glad and sincere hearts, praising God...and the Lord added to their number daily those who were being saved.* Many will be attracted to us as they see us meeting gladly and praising God together. You were not meant to praise God in isolation. Let us create our own valley of praise as we meet regularly in the assembly of God's people and echo the psalmist:

I will extol the Lord at all times; His praise will always be on my lips **(Ps 34v1).**

Chapter 7

The Fourth Man

Not long after the British Labour Party's 13 years in power from 1997-2010 came to an end one of their number published his memoirs entitled 'The Third Man'. This was a reference to his presence working behind the scenes helping the two most prominent people in the party who both served as British Prime Minister. Often when we see people in the frontline of politics or other roles in public view there is another visible personality working to influence what happens to them.

There is an occasion in the Bible when three men experienced a difficult situation in public view and were helped by a visible fourth man who influenced what happened to them. This incident is recorded in Daniel chapter 3. It is at a time when King Nebuchadnezzar of Babylon decreed that everyone fall down and worship at the appointed times a ninety feet gold statue of himself. Three men from the exiled nation of Israel refused to do so. Their names were Shadrach, Meshach and Abednego. Their story is the story of 'The Fourth Man'.

When the three friends were thrown into a blazing furnace as punishment, Nebuchadnezzar was so angry with them that the furnace was heated seven times hotter than usual. This was all for just staying true to the God of Israel and not worshipping the gods of Babylon or an image of gold. I'm sure we've experienced times when all we seem to be doing is honouring

God in our lives only for things to get even worse. This was the reality facing Shadrach, Meshach and Abednego.

When they were in the fiery furnace Nebuchadnezzar looks on and makes a startling observation which forces him to leap to his feet and to ask his advisers in total amazement:

"Weren't there three men that we tied up and threw into the fire?" They replied, "Certainly, O King." **(Dan 3v24)**.

Nebuchadnezzar continued:

"Look! I see four men walking around in the fire, unbound and unharmed, and the fourth looks like a son of the gods" **(v.25)**.

One of the most mind blowing scenes in history is described as the three faithful Israelites leave the fire behind:

Nebuchadnezzar then approached the opening of the blazing furnace and shouted, "Shadrach, Meshach and Abednego, servants of the Most High God, come out! Come here!"

So, Shadrach, Meshach and Abednego came out of the fire and the satraps, prefects, governors and royal advisers crowded around them. They saw that the fire had not harmed their bodies, nor was a hair of their heads singed; their robes were not scorched and there was no smell of fire on them **(vv.26-27)**.

Nebuchadnezzar arrives at the conclusion:

no other god can save in this way **(v.29)**

Another affirmation of this is found in

Isaiah 43v2 *when you pass through the waters, I will be with you; and when you pass through the rivers, they will not sweep over you, when you walk through the fire, you will not be burned; the flames will not set you ablaze.*

Now I'm not recommending that Christians throw themselves into a burning fire to see what happens. We should not go looking for the fire but neither should we pretend that our faith will not be tested and we need to prepare for the heat to be turned up at different points in our faith journey:

Now for a little while you have had to suffer grief in all kinds of trials. These have come so that your faith - of greater worth than gold, which perishes even though refined by fire - may be proved genuine and may result in praise, glory and honour when Jesus Christ is revealed **(1 Peter 1v6b-7)**.

When the Refiner's fire visits us as it surely will we may find it helpful to draw on some lessons which can be learned from the example of Shadrach, Meshach and Abednego.

Avoid Defensive manoeuvres

The last thing the three of them felt the need to do was defend themselves. They knew they had been faithful to God; they had not bowed the knee to idols. They were confident that they were at the centre of God's will and their consciences were clear. They acted as if God was pleased with them and this released them from the fear of man. They did not try to come up with a winning argument to gain the king's sympathy or convince him they were in the right. Living at the centre of God's will empowers us with great freedom. We move away from self-condemning thoughts and are not weighed down by the accusations of others. In this type of scenario God's opinion is the only one we're interested in and we lose the pressure of trying to convince anyone that we are in the right. We realise God is watching and we feel His pleasure over us. Shadrach, Meshach and Abednego were secure in God's love for them and delight in them. Are we relishing in God's pleasure of us and how He delights in us?

Psalm 147v11 *the Lord delights in those who fear him, who put their hope in his unfailing love.*

Don't look so surprised

We have touched on this already in the acceptance that our faith will be tested but we can still have a begrudging acceptance of this and so become very indignant during times of testing as if something strange were happening to us:

1 Peter 4v12 *Dear friends, do not be surprised at the painful trial you are suffering, as though something strange were happening to you.*

2 Timothy 3v12 *in fact, everyone who wants to live a godly life in Christ Jesus will be persecuted.*

Shadrach, Meshach and Abednego expressed no indignant surprise at what was unfolding. They knew they had gone against the wishes of the king and fully anticipated this would not go down well. There is a sense of 'so be it' at the beginning of their statement in **Dan 3v17** *if we are thrown into the blazing furnace*. They were resigned to the reality that if you do God's will forces are at work to oppose this. Recently I have been rising earlier in the morning to spend more time in prayer at the outset of the day. I have found this immensely rewarding in many ways and seen numerous answers to prayer linked to it. However, I have also discovered that the enemy does not want me doing this and has conspired to make me ill and more tired physically so that I return to lying in bed a bit longer in the mornings. What has helped me combat the enemy's assault in this is that I fully expected it – I prepared myself not to be surprised and this has actually strengthened me and spurred me on to continue praying – I have discovered the God who is never surprised helps those who embrace the inevitability of the battles Christians face. Like Shadrach, Meshach and Abednego let's not jump up and down in surprise as if fiery trials were something no one told us about. They are not alien to our walk with God; they are in fact a vital part of it.

God is able

The three friends had settled the issue that nothing is impossible for God. **V.17** *if we are thrown into the blazing furnace, the God we serve is able to save us from it*. The blazing furnace was met with a blazing faith in what God could do. They were faced with a big problem but they had a big vision of a big God. Perhaps we need to enlarge our vision of God. Are we limiting what He can do?

Recently my 9 year old son was playing on his snooker table in his bedroom. I was downstairs when he came to me and told me he had knocked his light bulb with his snooker cue and now it wasn't working. When I went upstairs and had a look at it I observed that the bulb had been smashed and was, therefore, beyond my ability to repair. It struck me that although I couldn't fix the problem immediately (I knew I could replace the broken bulb with a new one at the next opportunity) my son still came and told me about the problem because as his Dad he believed that I could do something about it. There are times when I don't feel very capable. But it is encouraging that a nine year old boy sees his dad as having a bigger ability than the problem facing him.

As believers in Christ we have become children of God (see John 1v12) and we must trust that our Dad (God) is bigger and stronger than any set of circumstances facing us.

In Matthew's gospel chapter 9 two blind men seek out Jesus. When they find him and ask for mercy, Jesus asks *them* a question, *"Do you believe that I am able to do this?"* (v.28). When they replied in the affirmative Jesus healed them in accordance with their faith (vv.28-9). Perhaps the Holy Spirit is speaking to you right now as you read these words. You are in the midst of a fiery trial that seems unbearable and has been lingering for some time. Ask the Holy Spirit to help you trust afresh that your God is for you and He is able to do more than what you have believed Him for.

The apostle Paul faced many life threatening situations and was able to declare,

He has delivered us from such a deadly peril, and he will deliver us. On him we have set our hope that he will continue to deliver us **(2 Cor. 1v10)**.

Whatever you're going through God is able to deliver you through this latest trial. Be encouraged to press on and set your hope on this 'Fourth Man' (God) who is our Deliverer. After the Lord had delivered David from his enemies he wrote Psalm 18 where he refers to God affectionately as *My Deliverer* **(Ps 18v2)**. We need to settle this issue that God -our Deliverer- is able.

God is sovereign

Shadrach, Meshach and Abednego understood that God is sovereign. After asserting that God was able to save them they told Nebuchadnezzar that even if He didn't they still wouldn't worship Babylonian gods or the statue of the king (Dan. 3v18). This illustrates their rest in the sovereignty of God by what I call follow through – i.e. even if we do go through the fiery furnace and get burned 'we are not for turning'.

The former British Prime Minister Margaret Thatcher was known as The Iron Lady and famously stated "the Lady's not for turning" as she made unpopular decisions she believed right for the nation.

If we believe that we are taking the right God honouring course of action in a given situation then we are led to 'follow through' and are not for turning even when the results may invite opposition.

So, it's not about whether God rescues us or not, it's about knowing God controls our destiny and that He has a sovereign purpose.

Rom. 8v28 *and we know that in all things God works for the good of those who love Him, who have been called according to his purpose.*

This means God is sovereignly working for our good even if it means fiery trials. When we get revelation about the sovereignty of God it gives us 'sight beyond sight', that is, sight beyond what we see before us. This kind of sight looks for that 'Fourth Man' in the fire and finds Him.

Unconditional Surrender

The unswerving commitment of the three exiles spoke volumes to Nebuchadnezzar.

Daniel 3v28 *Then Nebuchadnezzar said, "Praise be to the God of Shadrach, Meshach and Abednego, who has sent his angel and rescued His servants! They trusted in Him and defied the King's command and were willing to give up their lives rather than serve or worship any god except their own God...."*

Interestingly, it seems that the king was as much impacted by their willingness to give up their lives as he was by their actual rescue.

Are we impacting others who are struck by our devotion to God? We can either look like people who are wholeheartedly surrendered to God's will or those who have attached conditions?

Towards the end of WW2 the United States knew from intercepted messages between Tokyo and Moscow that the Japanese were seeking a *conditional* surrender. American policy-makers, however, were not inclined to accept a Japanese "surrender" that left its military dictatorship intact and even possibly allowed it to retain some of its wartime conquests.

God is not inclined to accept *conditional* surrender from us which leaves intact an attitude of dictating to Him which part of our lives He can control and which strongholds we will not relinquish.

An Old Testament character who was an expert at doing almost all of God's will was King Saul. On one occasion he is said to have *acted foolishly* in making a burnt offering before the prophet Samuel had arrived. Saul panicked because the troops were beginning to scatter and Samuel had not come at exactly the set time (see **1 Samuel 13**). Later on the final straw comes when Saul hoards some of the spoils from victory against God's clear instruction through the prophet (Samuel) that everything belonging to the enemy was to be destroyed (1 Samuel 15).Tragically, Saul continued in this vein for the rest of his days.

Doing almost all of God's will is something many Christians can seem to live with. It's time to move away from this position. God is scouting for a people who desire Him so much that the idea of *conditional* surrender becomes repulsive. Be open to the Holy Spirit to demolish strongholds where we may still be dictating to God the level of our commitment. Let's aim for more than doing *almost* all of God's will and become familiar instead with the concept of *unconditional* surrender.

Conscious of God

The thoughts outlined in this chapter could be placed under the umbrella question, Are you conscious of God?

> **1 Peter 2v19** *For it is commendable if a man bears up under the pain of unjust suffering because he is conscious of God.*

Being conscious of God with us in the midst of trials enables us to go through the fire and bear the pain, even if the pain seems unjustified. Shadrach, Meshach and Abednego were three men very conscious of God, represented by the 'Fourth Man' in the fire.

It is one of my key purposes in writing that we hunger for being more conscious of God's presence. Let this hunger itself become a fire that consumes us. In this high pursuit I pray we not only discover the Fourth Man in the fire but encounter many astonished Nebuchadnezzars along the way who say something like, "Look! I see them walking around in the fire, unbound and unharmed".

Chapter 8

That Canaanite Woman

During the earthly ministry of Jesus he encountered a woman from Canaan (an old name for Palestine); an area not part of the Jewish world which Jesus had been prioritizing. This represented a barrier which required her to press in on Jesus if she wanted his attention.

A Desperate Situation

In **Matthew chapter 15** we read how the woman approached Jesus seeking mercy for her daughter, described as *suffering terribly from demon possession* (see v21). The Gospel of Mark's account tells us she was a little girl – so probably very young. I'm a father of four children myself and understand the distress any parent might feel when one of their children is even slightly unwell. There can be a sense of helplessness in these situations and the longer it continues the more desperate parents become to see improvement. So, this little girl was having her life ruined by a terrible affliction. She was suffering a lot and so in turn was her mother watching it all helplessly. A desperate situation I'm sure you'll agree.

Perhaps you feel as though your life is being ruined by an affliction or circumstances that you have no control over. You may have reached a point of total desperation. Often God allows us to get to this point knowing that we are more inclined to give up on our own efforts and finally give Him the opportunity to act.

Make some noise

The Canaanite woman came to Jesus, crying out, *Lord, Son of David, have mercy on me* (**Mt 15v22**). It's a similar cry to the two blind men near Jericho who heard Jesus was passing by and shouted, *Lord, Son of David, have mercy on us*! (**Mt 20vv29-32**). Now of course the Bible makes clear that God sees and knows everything and so we don't need to cry or shout at Him to get noticed. Yet, God often allows situations to play out where He already knows the outcome. For example, when the blind men outside Jericho called to Jesus he asked them what they wanted him to do for them (**Mt 20v32**). He already knew they wanted to see and that he would grant their request.

So why does God allow situations to get so desperate before stepping in. The answer is found in God's desire to reveal Himself in our daily circumstances. In these He seeks to reveal His mercy and power and will stop in His tracks when such an occasion presents itself. This way God alone gets the glory and is seen for who He is – a just God who will do what is right.

It might be time for you to exercise faith like that Canaanite woman and make some noise which causes God to stop and address your need. When I am in the house with my children I do not go running to see what they want all the time. If, though, one of them starts crying this arrests my attention immediately and I will not move on to do something else until I find out what's wrong and address it. Exercise your faith loudly, make some noise like that Canaanite woman and see what happens.

Create a disturbance

At first nothing seems to change. Jesus doesn't answer, not a single word. He gives her the silent treatment (**Mt 15v23**). But the persistent Canaanite woman is not so easily put off. She continues crying after Jesus and his disciples. This person is not going to slip quietly away and leave empty-handed. The persistence shown here unsettles the disciples with Jesus. They urge Jesus to do something about that Canaanite woman who was creating a disturbance and holding things up for Jesus and those travelling with him. Going further than making some noise to get God's attention we can be inspired by that Canaanite woman to really make a nuisance of ourselves before God (in a positive way) which draws him to meet with us at our point of need – **Heb.11v6b** *He rewards those who earnestly seek Him.* Let me encourage you to approach God with boldness which says you're not going away empty-handed. This attitude is entirely Biblical as we can see here. Consider also how Jacob wrestled with God through the night declaring, *I will not let you go unless you bless me* (**Gen 32vv25-6**).

To demonstrate this attitude does not mean we lack humility or that we are 'naming and claiming' as if we can demand something from God as our right. Rather, it is an attitude which understands God our Father doesn't mind being pestered by His children, in fact, Jesus actively encouraged this. In **Mt 18vv1-8** Jesus tells The Parable of the Persistent Widow about a widow who kept bothering a judge for justice. The lesson is summed up in **vv7-8**

And will not God bring about justice for His chosen ones, who cry to Him day and night? Will He keep putting them off? I tell you, He will

see that they get justice, and quickly. However, when the Son of
Man comes, will he find faith on the earth?

So keep crying out, finding your faith to create a disturbance and
the God of justice will see that such a display of faith is rewarded.

In my job I often deal with people who raise an issue that they want
dealt with. I have to encourage them that they are not bothering my
employers if they keep pestering them with their 'issue'. From
experience I know this is the best way to eventually get a
satisfactory response. The people I work for will divert extra
resources to ongoing issues which keep being brought to their
attention. Let's create a disturbance and keep diverting God's
attention towards our call for assistance. Don't be afraid to remind
God of His promise to bring justice to His people – He likes to be
reminded!

Kneeling

The Canaanite woman moves from crying and making a fuss to,
ultimately, kneeling before Jesus whilst reducing her plea simply to
Lord, help me (**Mt 15v25**). She calls Jesus *Lord* and bows the knee
accordingly. She is at the end of herself and has no words left to
utter other than Lord, help me. Jesus had broken his silence but still
had issued a further seemingly negative response in telling the
woman there were other needs to address before hers (*the lost
sheep of Israel* **v25**). At that point she could've lost hope completely
and concluded God wasn't interested. This attitude which resembles
a child throwing toys out of the pram is always a real temptation

when God doesn't dance to our tune. To the eternal credit of the Canaanite woman she recognised in faith that Jesus is Lord over every situation. She bows the knee in humble submission. Are we submitted to the Lordship of Jesus? It may be that we are in a process at the moment of God dealing with us in this area. If so, we must bend to the Holy Spirit who reveals Jesus to us more and more. We must trust in him alone as the one who helps us. The Canaanite woman exercises faith which looks one way. I urge us to look one way for help. The psalmists look to one person as our help. **Ps 46v1** *God is...an ever-present help in trouble.* **Ps 118v7** *He is my helper.* We need to allow the Holy Spirit to focus our eyes on Jesus in the midst of trouble and to look one way for help.

Ps 121v1-2 *I lift up my eyes to the hills- where does my help come from? My help comes from the Lord, the Maker of heaven and earth.*

Look to Jesus, he will help those who in faith proclaim him Lord and focus on him as the one who helps us, not focusing on the reason we need help. Let's look to the Lord our Helper in good times and in bad.

Eat the crumbs

Jesus restates his priority to help first the people of Israel who have lost their way (v26 *the dogs*). The woman does concede this (v27 *yes Lord*) but adds that she will be happy with the crumbs from the ministry of Jesus (see v27). That Canaanite woman will take whatever is on offer from Jesus. If I open a biscuit tin when I'm not particularly hungry and find only crumbs I may close the lid again and walk away without tasting anything. If, on the other hand, I'm really hungry I will taste some crumbs. I believe God looks for a hunger in each of us which means we're happy to eat the crumbs from the Master's table. God has more than crumbs to give us but is drawn to hearts happy to receive whatever He offers.

Show some faith

To summarise here, we must guard against an unhelpful mindset which compares ourselves to biblical characters like the Canaanite woman who appear to show great faith and we are left feeling we don't measure up and never can. Jesus encouraged his listeners to exercise mustard seed faith which starts as the smallest of garden seeds and grows to become the largest of garden plants. This mustard seed faith can be used by God to move mountains (see **Mt 17v20 ref Mt 13v31-32**). No Christian has a greater degree of mustard seed faith than another; it's just that some in the church are seen to exercise this mustard seed faith more than others. That Canaanite woman is seen to exercise faith, not great faith, just faith. She was an ordinary person just like us. If she can exercise faith, so can you!

Chapter 9

A Time to Straighten Up

Jesus labels our spiritual adversary the devil (or Satan) as *a liar and the Father of lies* (**Jn 8v44**). One of the ways he lies to Christians is by leading them to believe they should just accept their negative predicament without expecting anything to change in the near future. This may refer to a health battle, unhappy work life, relationship issues or something else which is pushing them to breaking point. If we let the lie in at the door that nothing will ever change then this takes a foothold in our thinking. The Bible directs us to avoid giving the devil a foothold (**Eph 4v27**). If we entertain the lies at the foothold stage they take an ever deeper hold as if we were being seized and thrown about by a force seeking to devour us (**1 Pet 5v8**). Eventually, if we do not throw off the lies of Satan seizing us in this way it builds a stronghold in our lives which leaves us bent over so that we are no longer looking straight ahead at the plans God has for us. This situation requires tearing down. The good news is that, in Christ, we have weapons to break free and demolish strongholds.

Divine weapons

2 Cor 10v3-5 is a bible passage which has been brought to the forefront of my mind often in various circumstances:

For though we live in the world, we do not wage war as the world does. The weapons we fight with are not the weapons of the world. On the contrary, they have divine power to demolish strongholds. We demolish arguments and every pretension that sets itself up against the knowledge of God, and we take captive every thought to make it obedient to Christ.

If more Christians refused to entertain the lying voices opposed to God at work within us, then many more in the church today would be walking straight and tall in God's grace and power, thus not so weighed down by circumstances and feelings of fear, guilt and condemnation.

The Truth Struggle

In the world of fantasy and science fiction authors and movie makers tell stories around the battles for supremacy between the forces of good and evil. For a long time as a Christian I operated as though I was involved with a power struggle between God and Satan. Now I realise that Christians are not involved in a power struggle but rather a truth struggle. The Bible stresses that Jesus triumphed over all powers and authorities when he willingly allowed himself to be crucified for our sake (see **Col 2v15**). His sacrifice satisfied once for all God's just requirement that a perfect penalty for sin (our wrongs) be paid (see **Heb 7v27b; 1 Pet 3v18; 1 Jn 2v2**). **Rom 6v11** tells us that because of this we are to now *count* ourselves or 'reckon it true' that we are *dead to sin but alive to God in Christ Jesus*. Because of Jesus we are now free to live in a position of being reconciled in relationship to God. Jesus said if we live in this truth of being set free in him, then the truth will set us free (see **Jn 8v32**). Unfortunately, many remain bent over and captive as if unaware of this awesome liberating truth. God wants us to act on what we know to be true. Although the devil is still active and looks for ways to keep us down he knows he is a defeated foe and that God has limited his power and set an appointed time for his ultimate destruction (**Rev 20v10**). One of the apostle Paul's concluding remarks to the church at Rome was *the God of peace will soon crush Satan under your feet* (**Rom 16v20**).

Of course it's not always a straightforward matter of speaking God's truth over circumstances and seeing instant results. Yet, if we refocus our gaze on the truth of our knowledge of God revealed in Jesus the lies of the enemy are eventually outmanoeuvred and overcome. The apostle Peter added his voice to Paul's in urging us to apply our knowledge of God's truth in Christ:

His divine power has given us everything we need for life and godliness through our knowledge of him who called us by his own glory and goodness (**2 Pet 1v3**).

Renewed Thinking

It's hard to act differently and see different results when every thought is poisoned at the source. One of the most significant transfers that takes place when we exchange the lies of God opposed voices for the truth of God's grace revealed in Jesus Christ is transformed thinking. The poisonous lies of the enemy are washed away by the knowledge of God's unfailing love for each one of us in Christ. In the context of being spiritually made knew in Christ Paul told the church at Ephesus *you were taught....to be made knew in the attitude of your minds* (**Eph 4v22, 23**).

Transformed thinking was a constant theme in Paul's teaching and we see it highlighted again in his thoughts to the believers at Rome:

> *Do not conform any longer to the pattern of this world, but be transformed by <u>the renewing of your mind</u>. Then you will be able to test and approve what God's will is – his good, pleasing and perfect will* (**Rom 12v2** emphasis added).

Conforming to the world's pattern of thinking keeps us in a place of Captivity. Choosing Renewal of the Mind through Jesus brings us into a place of Freedom.

Captivity or Freedom

At the outset of his earthly ministry Jesus quoted the prophet Isaiah and underlined his own core mission to among other things *proclaim freedom for the prisoner, recovery of sight for the blind* and *release* for *the oppressed* (**Luke 4v18**).

Further along in his ministry journeys whilst teaching in one of the synagogues Jesus encounters a woman who is physically *bent over and could not straighten up at all* (**Luke 13v10-11**). The text suggests she was in a place of captivity and oppression through this condition. We learn this as Jesus refers to Satan having kept her _bound_ _for eighteen long years_ (**v16**). The woman needed what a lot of us can receive from Jesus; Freedom from what is keeping us bound and Release from what we are allowing to oppress us.

Once I injured my back quite badly and was bent over for several days not able to straighten up. I had to take a week off work. I spent a lot of time looking down and not much time looking up or straight ahead. I was limited in the everyday activities I would usually manage without difficulty. Happily, the condition was temporary and I did eventually recover. However, when I visited a physiotherapist as part of my recovery I was told that it was a mistake to stop exercising altogether as this would make the back seize up even more. I was shown exercises designed to get the movement going again in the affected area and had I been given this knowledge sooner my recovery would've been faster.

If we are in difficulty at present, feeling bent over with all the pressure and not able to straighten, God is looking to visit us and minister healing and truth in the name of Jesus. If we want to recover it's no good retreating quietly into the shadows and just hoping things will eventually improve. This will only cause our life in God to seize up even more and prolong our recovery. Progress will be much faster if we visit the truth surgery of Jesus and listen to his life changing advice to our hearts and minds. Jesus sees our pain and does not choose to ignore it.

He calls you forward

After Jesus sees the woman, we are told the first thing he does is call her forward (**Lk 13v11**). This suggests she was holding back from Jesus, lingering in the background, possibly feeling Jesus had others around him to be more concerned about. It's likely she had become so accustomed to her condition leaving her on the margins of society that she felt unworthy to seek an audience with Jesus – and why should he treat her any different than anyone else who came across her.

A woman in my local church recently shared her experience at school of always being the last or one of the last to be chosen by other pupils to be in their team for sports activities. This was because she wasn't particularly good at sports. So, she would be left in a line waiting to be called out or called forward as the names of others kept getting chosen before her. This kind of experience in childhood can really stay with a person and I could sense this was the case with this woman in our church who told the story. I now recall others in my own school years that no one was in a hurry to call forward from line-ups for sports teams. I wonder how deeply it affected them.

Jesus is in the habit of calling people forward; the poor, the marginalised, the hurting, those who others try to avoid, can't help or have given up on. Jesus is interested in you whoever you are and whatever your circumstances, whether you appear to have it all together or feel totally inadequate for anything. Jesus calls you forward. He wants to interact with you, to meet you at your point of need. In his earthly ministry Jesus went out of his way to call people forward: the blind beggar (**Lk 18**); Zacchaeus (**Lk 19**) the insignificant looking and hated tax collector; Lazarus (**Jn 11**) – who by the way was dead at the time. Reader, listen to the heart of Jesus: he calls you forward. Wherever you are and whatever state you're in.

Lies, lies, Lies

The writer of Luke's gospel records that is was Satan not God who had kept the disabled woman in bondage for eighteen long years. The paradox is God allows it but Satan sends it. It is Satan who wants to keep us bound, not God. We need to get perspective on this. Many in the church choose to remain bent over whether this is physically, spiritually, or emotionally and decide somehow that God is ok with this. They become a kind of prisoner in their own lives having convinced themselves this is the specific will of God for them. Lies, lies, lies!!! Has God told us He wants prisoners? You will not find that anywhere in the Bible. Rather God has proclaimed in Jesus, 'freedom for the prisoners'.

During wartime soldiers get captured by the enemy. Some are driven by a sense of duty to try to break free from captivity, whilst others sit back and wait to be rescued. The bent over woman Jesus encountered was looking down and not seeing things clearly. Jesus saw her and was clear that God's purpose for her was not captivity but freedom. It's not God's will for you to sit back and remain depressed, anxious, or just struggling through each day. God in Christ has called us forward to a higher level of living:

Jn 10v10 *The thief comes only to steal and kill and destroy; I have come that they may have life, and have it to the full.*

The word of freedom

The first thing Jesus said to the woman was a word of freedom; *women you are set free from your infirmity* (**Lk 13v12**).

It wasn't just what Jesus did that made such an impact on those who heard about him and followed him; it was also his words, his amazing, life changing words.

There's a scene in the multi-award-winning movie 'Ben Hur' when the fictional hero sees Jesus carrying the cross. He remembers meeting him before when he was down and out and remarks about this Jesus that "he gave me the heart to live". Ben Hur follows Jesus to the place of crucifixion then returns home after Jesus dies. He tells the woman waiting for him what Jesus said about those who crucified him; *Father forgive them for they know not what they do* (ref **Luke 23v34**). At this point, both Ben Hur and the woman he's telling this to are totally awestruck that Jesus spoke these words even after all the evil that had been done to him at the hands of man. Ben Hur says also that these words took the sword from his hand meaning they had pierced him and removed the violent anger and hatred he felt towards Rome.

This fictional scene taps into the real truth that the words of Jesus penetrate to the core of human hearts. Consider the impact some of his words had on his hearers;

Luke 19v48 - *all the people hung on his words;*

Luke 24v32 – *were not our hearts burning within us while he talked with us on the road and opened the scriptures to us?*

Jn 4v41 - *and because of his words many more became believers*

Jn 8v30 – *even as he spoke, many put their faith in him*

The point I make here is that when God sees your need and sees your struggle to keep pressing on, by His Spirit He draws near to speak words of freedom like he did to the disabled woman. Listen as God gives you a heart to live, as He speaks the words of freedom, life, strengthening, forgiveness and hope.

After Jesus spoke the word of freedom to the woman, she did something in response.

Straighten up

The Bible doesn't say that Jesus lifted the woman up or pulled her up straight. Although Jesus was clearly ministering healing power to her this does not negate her conscious decision to straighten up. When I sit at a desk studying I can without thinking bend over more and more until I'm virtually hunched over the desk. This is not good for my posture and I need to make a conscious decision to straighten up and avoid serious strain to my back, particularly since I've weakened it in the past as I referred to earlier.

In the Christian life pressures we come under can leave us bent over. God wants to minister change to this situation but He also expects us to make a conscious decision to straighten up. The disabled woman didn't just hear the word of freedom spoken over her by Jesus; she acted on it. James, a leader in the early church wrote *don't just hear the word, do what it says* (**James 1v22**). The disabled woman responded to God's concern for her need. She maximised the moment, believed God and put the word of freedom into practice. She straightened up as God enabled her. With God's help, we can do the same.

Chapter 10

Keeping up Appearances

This was the title of a very popular situation comedy on British television during the first half of the 1990s. According to Wikipedia it centred on an eccentric, social-climbing snob Hyacinth Bucket (who insists that her surname is pronounced Bouquet). She desperately tries to hide the fact that she was born into the working class. If people find out about this, she will automatically lose her 'middle class' status. The character is obsessed by perfection, image and etiquette.

Today, we live in an image-conscious society – particularly in the western world. People are constantly trying to present an image of themselves which they want others to believe is the real them which, most of the time, it isn't. We can all become victims of this image-obsessed culture in our striving for more money, a bigger house or better car as status symbols. We also live in the age of home computers and the latest 'must have' gadgets (high tech mobile phones and electronic reading machines). This has given rise to so-called social networking sites as Facebook and Twitter, where again people create their own virtual image of themselves with particular photos and comments. I'm writing these words as we approach Christmas time once again and although I speak to people who say they're fed up with how commercialised it has become many end up spending too much money as they feel pressure to live up to the image of what is expected as part of the Christmas merry-go-round. Now, I'm not saying this is how everyone operates but even those who don't can feel like second-class citizens if they don't follow the hype and live up to the image society has created.

Sometimes people project an image that all is well to deflect from issues going on in their lives. If I come across this I want to say "will the real you please stand up". I don't of course because none of us are perfect and I'm on a continuing journey myself of adjustment. However, it is important to be real about who we are and what type of people we should be for true genuineness and sincerity to be evident in our relationships with others. Our everyday experiences do not match the picture postcard image we often project to others and we must be set free from striving to uphold that image. Currently, I live in the Lake District area of Cumbria, England, which is full of a lot of beautiful scenery. There are, though, areas which look run down and in need of development. You will not see those areas on postcards which holiday makers send to relatives.

For the Christian, it is clear in the teachings of Jesus he looks not at how things appear on the outside but rather what is the state of our hearts before God. Jesus calls the religious leaders of his day '*whitewashed tombs*', looking beautiful on the outside but on the inside full of dead men's bones and everything unclean (see Matthew 23v7). We can have this kind of approach to being a Christian, projecting an outward appearance of all being well when inside our hearts are not right before God. This can remain true for those who are already followers of Jesus. It's easy to become distracted by goals of praying regularly, reading our bibles, attending church meetings, giving up certain habits we deem incompatible with the Christian life. Whilst these pursuits should be part of our Christian experience we can fall in to the trap of just saying and doing what we think is expected of a Christian whilst our heart relationship with God is neglected.

Measuring Motivation

The question we need to ask ourselves is what motivates us? This goes to the core of what is going on within us, individually and corporately as churches. Why are we doing what we are doing? Many shops specialize in window dressing. An attractive shop front window display is aimed at causing the potential customer to stop and venture inside. I've entered shops which don't live up to the quality of the window display. Sound familiar? We can dress our lives up to make people stop and stare and think that looks impressive. However, if they delved more deeply or got to know us better they may be disappointed. Churches similarly can focus on having the best worship band, dynamic preaching and multiple ways of engaging with the surrounding community. On the surface it appears all is well and there is a buzz of activity. On closer inspection something is missing. What could it be? Often, it is a lack of vulnerability and reality in the relationships of the people meeting together. To avoid this being honest with ourselves and God is vital. Otherwise we carry on wearing a mask of spiritually which gives a misleading picture of what is truly going on.

The Pharisee and the Tax Collector

In Luke's gospel chapter 18 the writer draws a parallel between an outwardly religious person who shouts about it from the rooftops whilst looking down on others and a person who realises their own spiritual poverty without God and who throws themselves on God's mercy. God looks for the latter. Elsewhere in **Matthew chapter 5v3** Jesus is recorded to have said *blessed are the poor in spirit for theirs is the kingdom of heaven*. In other words happy are those who realise their own spiritually poverty-stricken state without God. They have the right heart attitude to be welcomed into God's everlasting kingdom. Returning to Luke, the outwardly religious person represented by the Pharisee points to those who try to earn God's pleasure through self-effort and proudly boast about it as if displaying some kind of spiritual merit badge. What God is after is more of the honesty displayed by the tax collector. The tax collector sees himself on the same level as adulterers, robbers or evildoers. For, he understands that in God's eyes we're all wrongdoers. **Romans 3v23** *all have sinned and fall short of the glory of God.* The tax collector comes to God as he is without a mask of pretence and invites God to accept him as he is. This is the sincere way all of us are challenged to approach God.

Real friendships

The bible tells the reader *apart from God we can do nothing* (**John 15v5**). Those who accept this are prepared to be vulnerable. Vulnerability is essential if we are to be real before God but is also fundamental for our relationships in the church.

A significant number of Christians try to tough it out through difficult times and in doing so will often grow more isolated from other believers in their fellowship. At the same time they keep up a mask of spirituality when they do come into contact with others in the church. If we're struggling, however, we need to say so instead of acting in denial and deceiving both ourselves and others in the process. When the apostle Paul writes to the church at Ephesus he advises them to *put off falsehood and speak truthfully* to one another (see **Eph 4v5**). Jesus said *out of the overflow of the heart the mouth speaks* (**Matthew 12v34**). In our hearts we must prepare to be honest and real with one another. The people of God need to heed the warning of Isaiah: *truth has stumbled in the streets, honesty cannot enter. Truth is nowhere to be found* (**Isaiah 59v14-15**). When the music and preaching stops is truth and honesty found in the corridors of our fellowship? The real question is perhaps how well do we really know one another?

The antidote to pretence

According to the bible right standing before God is not achieved by us, it is a free gift of God's grace revealed in his son Jesus Christ:

John 3v16 *For God so loved the world that he sent his one and only son, that whoever believes in him shall not perish but have eternal life.*

It's all about what God has done in sending Jesus. In doing this God made the first move when we were in a hopeless position:

Isaiah 64v6 *all our righteous acts are as filthy rags to God.*

So any boasting like the Pharisee which says look at me God and haven't I done well and earned your favour is utterly pointless. Being a good person or going about doing good deeds might earn us some recognition in this world but doesn't book us a place in heaven.

Ephesians 2v8-9 *For it is by grace you have been saved, through faith* (in Christ) *- and this not from yourselves, it is the gift of God - not by works, so that no one can boast.*

The focus of the Christian life is not to be us and what we have done but rather God and what He has done. It is God Himself who freely gives us right standing before Him in Christ – something which we don't deserve and cannot earn. This is the absurdity of God's grace; giving us what we haven't earned and never could earn. Falling short of what God intended for His creation means we were deserving of His wrath and judgement but instead He revealed His desire for us to be restored into right relationship with Him:

Romans 5v8 *but God demonstrates His own love for us in this: While we were still sinners, Christ died for us.*

If we allow the grace of God in Jesus to enter our lives a daily reliance on it is our antidote to being false with others and pretending to be super-spiritual. Realising that God in His grace makes no distinction between us but accepts all who trust in Jesus leads us to abandon the pretence of 'keeping up appearances' and teaches us to stop distinguishing between ourselves and those we think don't measure up to a particular standard of living.

The Truth will out

Trying to play a part we think other people expect of us and in the hope of gaining some recognition will ultimately be our undoing. I once watched a movie entitled 'Picture Perfect' about a plainly dressed woman who works in an office but aspires towards greater recognition and opportunity from her employers. At first she doesn't know how to go about this until she was advised "you have to dress for the job you want". So, she sets about changing her image. She dresses sharper and begins saying all the right things to get her noticed. She manoeuvres towards a better position in the company. In the end, all her efforts unravel because the external self she has been putting out doesn't sit well with her internal self (the person she really is inside). She eventually confesses during a presentation in front of her bosses that she has been 'dressing for the job she wanted' and makes clear she doesn't want to keep doing this.

In the bible story of David and Goliath, David is dressed by King Saul in what everyone thinks David should wear to give him a fighting chance against the giant Philistine champion warrior Goliath who had put fear into all of Saul's army. David was a boy and not used to wearing heavy armour. He couldn't walk in it properly and be free to be himself so he took it off. Then he went out to meet the giant armed only with his stick, five smooth stones and a sling to fire them with. In other words, he went to meet Goliath as himself (see **1 Samuel 17v38-40**).

This episode in the bible resonates with me. If I'm in an environment where I don't feel free to be myself, I will look for the exit door. A church leader once said to me that he believed I had in the past been like David in Saul's armour. I knew this was true in my own life journey and that 'dressing in the armour' others put on me or expected me to wear had almost worn me out completely. It does us no good dressing in a manner that is uncomfortable with who we really are inside. We will not be able to sustain indefinitely the pretence that it fits us. God has a habit of keeping after our internal self until we stop running and admit the truth. The truth will come out in the end – it always does. As far as those in the church are concerned it's better not to be like David in Saul's armour. There is enough pretending in the world without people seeing it repeated in the church. True followers of Jesus should throw off the metaphorical masks, armour or whatever else hinders us being real with God, ourselves and fellow believers. In God's eyes all are equal. Perhaps we need to consider aligning ourselves with how God sees us and stop dressing to impress or as if we are auditioning for a part in a play. We will only change as we are convinced of the need for change. Pause and consider the pitfalls of keeping up appearances. Consider the bible's message of what matters to God - truth and humility in our relationship with Him and one another. As we do this and become people who are less false and more real we will be better equipped to keep pressing on.

Chapter 11

Making the right investment

A woman named Martha opened her home to Jesus (see Luke 10v38-42). At first glance this seems a very positive thing which she has done. She wants Jesus to feel as though he is welcome. However, Martha has an interesting approach to this. She gets distracted with preparations that 'have' to be made and it is in fact her sister Mary who sits down and begins listening to their guest. This raises the question of how we receive Jesus.

Distractions, Distractions

Martha gets distracted with tasks that she believes need addressing during the visit of Jesus. She burdens herself with self-imposed expectations. Jesus remarks to Martha that Mary has chosen what is better (see Luke 10v42), namely, that **being with** him is better than **doing for** him. According to the context of this situation we can understand how easily we get sidetracked by expectations we put on ourselves, expectations which do not come from Jesus. At this point, you might be thinking aren't we being a little unfair to Martha? After all, she only makes preparations that many of us would involve ourselves with if we had a guest to our home; surely she was being respectful in trying to make a bit of an effort.

A long-running British TV programme called 'Come Dine with me' shows people trying to outdo one another with food and atmosphere as each participant's home is visited in turn by the other guests on the show who then give a score afterwards.

Those who look to Jesus need to banish any thought that he is sitting with a score card rating our performance in how well we have entertained him or what efforts we have made to win his favour. Trying to outdo someone else or encouraging Jesus to be wowed by what a good job we've done can become a huge distraction. Although it is healthy to signal a warm welcome to Jesus in our hearts and minds, we must not get so sidetracked trying to please him that we are not really giving time to being still and waiting in his presence. He is pleased to just spend time with us as we pray and rest in him. This doesn't mean that we do nothing for him but rather that our relationship with him isn't determined by the extent of it. If we miss this then we can move further from where he wants us. The preparations Martha engaged in actually took her away from sitting at the feet of Jesus and being able to listen and converse with him effectively. Although Jesus was a guest in Martha's house, it was her (the host) who needed to receive from him (the guest), not the other way around.

Be where he wants you

Opening her home to Jesus gave Martha an opportunity to be nearer Jesus. Instead she remains at a distance as her busyness keeps her occupied. The end result is that Jesus is where Martha wants him but she is not where he wants her to be. Jesus looks to be invited into the home of our lives but we can allow him to just 'pop over for a visit' without really getting to know him. When guests are invited to my home they are going to feel uneasy if I spend most of the time they are in the house rushing around or being busy in the kitchen. If a guest is to be properly welcomed then I need to sit down and engage them in conversation. That is where a guest wants a host to be. Are we concerned with hosting Jesus properly?

Hang on I can't hear you

Quite often in our household what will happen is I will be in one room and my wife will be in another when she starts trying to have a conversation with me. In this situation I likely can't hear her clearly or concentrate on what she's saying as I'm either at the other end of the house or she is competing with the noise of the shower, washing machine or various other sounds. I then find myself calling out, "hang on I can't hear you" (or words to that effect). If I'm going to have an actual conversation with her I must move closer to where she is or vice-versa (usually my wife waits until I move to where she is). The writer James in the Bible urges us *come near to God and he will come near to you* (James 4v8). Martha needed to come closer to Jesus by laying aside the jobs she became distracted with. It's also possible that the preparations she was making were fairly noisy but in any case they keep her from hearing what Mary can hear sat as she is at the feet of Jesus. The situation grows more intolerable for Martha but not for the right reason.

Please recognise me

When Martha does get around to approaching Jesus she comes to him and asks, *Lord don't you care that my sister has left me to do the work by myself? Tell her to help me* (see Luke 10v40). Martha loses the plot a bit here. She has clearly grown increasingly upset that her busy efforts making everything ready for her guest appear to go unnoticed by Jesus. On top of that Jesus doesn't seem (from Martha's perspective) to care that her sister Mary is sat down at his feet whilst Martha is rushing around doing all the jobs on her own. Martha hasn't considered the problem may be her own inability and/or unwillingness to listen to Jesus. When she approaches Jesus she does anything but listen. Indeed, she snaps at Jesus and demands he makes Mary help her. You can almost hear a veiled threat 'tell Mary to help me or else'...or else what... 'Or else you can clear off or I'm out of here'. So the situation which Martha found intolerable was not that she couldn't hear Jesus but that she was being treated unfairly.

The elusive 'Well Done Certificate'

I have kept a number of so-named 'Well Done Certificates' that my children's junior school awarded them over the years for working hard in various subjects and in other ways. It's not a bad thing to have efforts recognised and everyone needs some encouragement. In fact just the other day my line manager at work sent me recognition for the good quality of service a particular member of the public said I had shown them.

However, a major problem arises when our own internal security or self-acceptance is measured by the number of 'well done certificates' or comments we receive from others. If we are not being patted on the back and told 'good effort' we become anxious and frustrated until this boils over to angry and abrupt responses towards those around us.

Jesus spelt it out for his audiences on earth that we do not earn our place in heaven like a day's wages (see Matthew 20 - the parable of the workers in the vineyard). Similarly, we do not earn any well done certificates for rushing around doing good works. Many who put their faith in Jesus respond initially to the message that he willingly died a death that we all deserved because of our inherent bias towards selfish acts; **Romans 6v23** *the wages of sin is death but the gift of God is eternal life in Christ Jesus our Lord.* The temptation though after accepting this message of God's forgiveness freely offered through Jesus is to add our own efforts for recognition on top of it. The message of the bible is that we are freed from this false pursuit as we trust completely in God's total acceptance of us through the gift of his son Jesus.

Pursuing this life of freedom in Jesus Christ doesn't mean that efforts to please God and do good works are of no consequence. The writer of 1st John tells us that we shouldn't just say we love people but offer them no practical help (see 1 Jn v17-18). James, a brother of Jesus and a leader in the early church, states *faith without deeds is dead* (James 2v26). When Peter is preaching at the house of Cornelius he mentions that whilst on earth Jesus *went around doing good* (Acts 10v38). So there should be some practical outworking of a faith that is genuine. Ultimately though our acceptance and security come from what God has done not what we do and we should walk in the assurance that God loves and accepts us, no matter what (see Romans 5v8).

Martha failed to grasp that Jesus accepted her no matter what. No matter if the house wasn't spotlessly clean before he arrived and a few items might be missing from the dining table. Jesus didn't care for Martha any less than he cared for Mary; he accepted them both the same; it wasn't about Mary being sat down and Martha rushing around. Martha had the chance to learn that this mattered nothing in the overall scheme of things. Only as she took this on board would she stop carrying so much weight on her shoulders and not be so ready to point the finger of accusation at others.

Only one thing is needed

If I'm being honest I have to say that a number of people who appear in church can be reluctant to appear that they need anything. Lip service is paid in songs and prayers to a need of Jesus but when it comes to relationship interaction with other church members it's easier to rush around pretending all is well than to slow down and risk revealing any needs or dependence. Not all fall into this category but it raises a genuine question for the church today: is there a willingness to stand still long enough to be honest with oneself and others? When I'm not happy or in a good state of mind it is usually obvious to others who observe me; it's obvious there's 'an elephant in the room'. I'm not great at hiding feelings and they usually reveal themselves when dealing with people. I have experienced real frustration when some in the church do not seem as open and when the going is obviously getting tough they decide to get busy rather than discuss what's bothering them. Martha got busy rather than embrace the only thing she really needed – to be still and rest in the person and presence of Jesus. We are not good at being still but when it comes to a relationship with God that very thing is really important. The psalmist understood this:

Psalm 46v10 *Be still and know that I am God*

Wear and tear

I once heard a church leader proclaim "worry will wear you out". When we get busy rather than deal with real issues in our lives (like Martha) we resemble a circus performer rushing around spinning many plates at the same time. This will cause us a great deal of worry and anxiety as we try to avoid plates falling and smashing. We will end up being *upset about many things* as Jesus pointed out to Martha (see Lk 10v41). This robs us of enjoying life and to coin a phrase we 'cannot see the wood for the trees'. Jesus was basically reminding Martha to get her priorities in order. Listening and responding to God among us is the main priority underlined here as it is throughout the bible. This main thing should override the many distractions which threaten to get in the way of it. So, Jesus is saying 'keep the main thing the main thing'. Martha chose the many things, Mary chose the main thing. According to Jesus, Mary chose *what is better* (Lk 10v42).

Many things will be taken away

In 1929 millionaires became paupers overnight when the stock market in the United States of America crashed. Wikipedia sums it up as "the most devastating stock market crash in the history of the United States, taking into consideration the full extent and duration of its fallout." A sharp quote about it reads

"Anyone who bought stocks in mid-1929 and held onto them saw most of his or her adult life pass by before getting back to even" – Richard M. Salsman

In the bible Paul writes to Timothy

Command those who are rich in this present world not to be arrogant nor to put their hope in wealth, which is so uncertain, but to put their hope in God (1 Tim 6v17).

You are free to make your choice about whether you believe the bible speaks the truth that sets us free or is just a load of made up nonsense. If though, as many millions the world over, you believe the former, then you benefit in heeding its message to make the right investment for the future; hope in God. There are a lot of people living with uncertainty because they have put their trust in the things of this world which are so uncertain. The Stock market is one example. Others which have come to the fore in the early 21st Century include the integrity of politicians, bankers and the media along with economic problems in eurozone countries. The claim of the bible is that trusting Jesus is the only firm foundation for this life and into eternity. The kingdom we enter into through faith in him is described as *a kingdom which cannot be shaken* (Heb 12v28).

Jesus taught that if we build our lives on anything else it's like investing in a house built on sand (see Matthew 7v24-27) which in stormy weather falls down with a 'great crash', leaving a deep impact.

On September 11th 2001 The Twin Towers in New York were hit by planes controlled by terrorists and despite their huge size and imposing presence they came crashing down like a deck of cards with the loss of many lives. World history is littered with similar tragic events.

In 1912 the 'unsinkable' Titanic hit an iceberg on its maiden voyage and sank within 2 hours. A major factor was that the iceberg warnings went unheeded. The bible is like a warning to us through the airwaves of our lives 'icebergs dead ahead'! Slow down, change pace, alter course! What kind of radio operators do we want to be? Will we heed the warning and avoid the Titanic Syndrome, sparing our lives further shipwreck and devastation? Life with Jesus at the helm does not promise plain sailing as he himself indicated:

John 16v33 *in this world you will have trouble*

Nevertheless it is a life filled with certainties; the verse above goes on to say *but take heart I have overcome the world* (Jn 16v33b).

Jesus told a story about people being invited to a great banquet and how one by one they made up excuses about how they had to deal with other stuff first before they could attend. These excuses actually lead to them missing out in the end (see Luke 14v15-24). They did not choose what is better. I encourage us to consider our choice at this point: a life with the firm foundation of Jesus at the centre or one filled with uncertainties. At the home of Mary and Martha Jesus indicates to both that it is not better to strive for a perfect performance as host at the expense of investing in relationship with him. In any case, her efforts would soon be forgotten once the food was gone and the guests had departed. It would've been better for Martha to put away her busyness and instead find greater fulfilment in listening to the voice of Jesus. Mary was told *she has chosen what is better and it will not be taken away from her* (Luke 10v42). The incentive for us is clear: choose what is better in knowing Jesus and keep pressing on in the certainty that it will not be taken away.

Chapter 12

Remember why you left Egypt

When in training for my current job, an instructor told the group that there would be days when we found it difficult and wondered why we were doing the job. I admit that whilst I mainly enjoy my job there have been occasions when I questioned whether or not it was the job for me. During these moments of doubt I have been spurred on by the memory of how unhappy I was in my last job and the reasons why I left it behind.

Israel is a nation that once left behind enslavement to ancient Egypt. The Bible indicates that for centuries the Egyptians worked the Israelites ruthlessly and made their lives bitter with hard labour. At one stage the Pharaoh even commanded midwives to kill every male child born to an Israelite woman (see Exodus 1). When Israel was finally free from the heavy yoke of Egyptian slavery the people rejoiced at first but were quick to grumble again as soon as their new situation brought fresh challenges. Things come to a head when Israel is at the threshold of the Promised Land, Canaan, and realise they must confront powerful enemies and large, well protected cities. The people appear to engage in selective amnesia as they look back to their time in Egypt with rose-tinted glasses and wish they were back there. Israel at this time is an example of reactions to avoid for those tempted to look back on Egypt (whatever that represents) when confronted by fresh challenges ahead.

Poor Eyesight

When Israel sent 12 spies to explore Canaan they all returned successfully but didn't all agree on the way forward (see Numbers 13). Only 2, Joshua and Caleb, gave a positive report along the lines that the mission of conquering the land was (with a little faith) achievable. The rest put it in the too hard to do box. Was it they who needed to improve their vision or Joshua and Caleb who needed a reality check? The negative 10 spies certainly only saw problems and dead ends ahead. They could not see further than this so in that regard could be said to have limited vision. Joshua and Caleb on the other hand saw with eyes of faith fixed on God who according to biblical record had led the nation this far. Negativity was for Joshua and Caleb a symptom of poor eyesight and a mindset to push away from.

Negative Self-image

We come across a rather tragic statement from the negative spies in Numbers 13v33: *we seemed like grasshoppers in our own eyes and we looked the same to them*. This points to a negative mindset with every thought poisoned at the source as the Israelites began to focus on their weak minded selves. So, as they face challenges all their basic insecurities about themselves come to the surface and they feel unable to move forward. They start making comparisons between themselves and the physically imposing Canaanite inhabitants. They see themselves in light of this and lose sight of how treasured they were by God who had so many good plans for them.

The overall negative view has a knock-on effect. If they had focused on what had already been overcome in getting this far then their feelings of inadequacy could've been managed. After all, their God had miraculously worked on their behalf to lead them from slavery and to humble the mighty Egyptians.

The Bible teaches that God does not see us as we see ourselves or through the eyes of others. Instead, He sees us through the finished work of His Son, Jesus Christ:

If anyone is in Christ, he is a new creation; the old has gone, the new has come (2 Corinthians 5v17).

A true Christian lives this out as a reality in everyday circumstances. The result is God-focused decision making not self-focused or people-focused deliberating. If you are reading this now I encourage you that the key to stepping forward towards a better future is bound up with knowing and responding to biblical revelation that each of us is unique and precious to God. We can be changed by the assurance that we are loved unconditionally with an endless and self-giving love:

For God so loved the world that He gave His one and only Son, that whoever believes in Him shall not perish but have eternal life (John 3v16).

Look at the birds of the air; they do not sow or reap or store away in barns and yet your heavenly Father feeds them. Are you not much more valuable than they (Matthew 6v26)?

God demonstrates His own love for us in this: While we were still sinners, Christ died for us (Rom 5v8).

Cast all your anxiety on Him because He cares for you (1 Peter 5v7).

The Israelites at the border of their Promised Land took their eye off the ball and lost sight of how precious they were to God. In fact, they behaved as if He had somehow abandoned them. Those who trust in God through faith in Christ discover that God never abandons us;

I will never leave you nor forsake you (Joshua 1v5)

I will not leave you as orphans (John 14v18)

Living with certainty that there is One who never abandons us is very empowering. It leads us away from this negative self-image. Which way are you heading: the Promised Land or back to Egypt? A negative self-image will not enable you to move in the right direction.

Fear of Loss

The Israelites were anxious (dare I say panicking) about what they might lose if they continued and pressed into Canaanite territory as opposed to anticipating what might be gained:

Our wives and children will be taken as plunder (Num. 14v3).

How often have we hesitated at a new opportunity due to concerns about what might be lost or taken away if we go ahead? Recently, I was speaking with some work colleagues about whether they would apply for advancement within the organisation as fresh vacancies had become available. One in particular who had waited years for such an opportunity was hesitant as it would involve losing out financially during the first year even though this would be reversed in the long-term.

I remember being in a church meeting once where the speaker told a story about a woman at a previous church gathering who had been doubled over and relied on a Zimmer frame. She allowed herself to be prayed for and spoke of how she felt healed afterwards. She straightened up and began to move about freely without any assistance. Then it was as if she caught herself in the process. Her joyous facial expression was seen to change to a worried one and she began to look sad. She returned to her Zimmer frame and began to move towards the exit of the building. The teller of this story recalled that by the time she left she had become hunched over again as if she had never experienced any improvement. It was as though she was struck by worry about the financial disability benefits she would surely lose if she became well.

The focus was again on fear of what would be lost rather than what would be gained through embracing change.

Someone once said that 'change' is the most dangerous word in the English vocabulary. It is true that it can give rise to both fear and excitement in equal measure. It does not serve us well if we allow fear to stop us seizing a new opportunity with better long-term prospects. The Israelites had cried out for change during the torment of their Egyptian enslavement. Unfortunately, they now cried out at what that change involved. They seemed blind to why they had cried out for change in the first place.

Those who trust God are challenged to give fears over to Him:

Cast all your cares and anxieties on Him (1 Pet 5v7 New Living Translation).

Don't be afraid; just believe (Mark 5v36).

Do not let your hearts be troubled. Trust in God (John 14v1).

A life of purpose with God at the helm directing us is a journey involving many changes. The perfect balance to this is that God through Christ remains the one constant who does not change:

Jesus Christ is the same yesterday and today and forever (Hebrews 13v8).

That guarantee can be an anchor within us. Only God can hold us steady when we are on the shifting ground of life's many changes and areas of new territory. We may feel the fear but the anchor overcomes this. A quote from adventurer and TV celebrity Bear Grylls puts it well:

Both faith and fear may sail into your harbour, but allow only faith to drop anchor.

If Only

When the nation of Israel saw the difficult road ahead they looked for an excuse to turn back. In doing so, they reverted to a default mode familiar to most of us: 'If Only'.

All the Israelites grumbled against Moses and Aaron and the whole assembly said to them, If only we had died in Egypt! Or in this desert (Num 14v2).

How often we default to these two words 'If only' as we react to the way ahead not being plain sailing; if only I had done better in school then I would have better prospects today; if only I had worked harder on my marriage then I wouldn't be divorced and feel so lonely; if only I had persevered in that last job or stayed living where I was before – it wasn't so bad after all. This 'if only' mentality looks back not forward and does not help us to keep pressing on with life's journey. It is a road to nowhere as we dwell on perceived missed opportunities or what might've been. Don't react to the unfamiliar by attempting to turn back the clock. Your Egypt is your past not your future. This is not an attempt to gloss over difficulties you may be facing. It's an attempt to underline that your past prepares you for what you're facing now. Life is a series of stages we go through and when one stage is passed it is necessary to move on. The past was a legitimate stage of your life but it was a building block for where you are now. If we jump ship because we don't like our present environment we will probably end up doing this at every stage for the rest of the journey.

The Israelites had left Egypt for good reason and God was after something better for His people. Unfortunately the people lost sight of this. Uncertainty led them to follow the signpost marked 'If only'. It will appear along the road for each one of us. To follow it is to chase after a past that we did well to leave behind.

The Despondent Society

The people of Israel on the whole formed themselves into one big crowd of despondent people. Like attracts like and those looking back to Egypt chatted among themselves so they could hear what they wanted to hear instead of what they needed to hear:

> *Wouldn't it be better for us to go back to Egypt? And they said to each other, we should choose a leader and go back to Egypt* (Num 14v3-4).

One can only speculate how the members of this despondent society talked up how much better life was in Egypt and how they could experience this again if they returned. This is a classic case of self-deception in order to avoid a new challenge. It breeds stubborn, fixed opinions that are stone deaf to objective advice. Even as this group looked to appoint a new leader who would support their cause, that leader would probably be dumped as soon as they disagreed with any future plans of this 'despondent society'.

As I alluded to earlier there have been days in my current job when I have been hit by waves of despondency. I know that the worst thing that can happen to me when I feel like this is to get around others who are also unhappy in the job. That feeds my despondency and only drives me further inward to find a solution which satisfies it. Not good. Agreeing with me and telling me what I want to hear at that time is not the objective advice I really need. If I make an important decision in this mindset it will be a poor decision based on self-deception not positive instruction. The Israel that got together and formed this band of discontents ended up making a poor decision. Their grumbling was the platform for a puppet leader who, if they got their way, would lead them out of doing the right thing. Despondency looks for a way out of doing the right thing. Good leadership does not facilitate this. There is nothing in the Bible to suggest that God facilitates it either.

The Disease is cured

There is a brief text in the Bible which haunts me:

Do everything without complaining or grumbling (Philippians 2v14).

We all encounter complaining and grumbling wherever we go today, whether it is poor service in a shop or being stuck in traffic. The problem with grumbling is that it spreads like a disease infecting a person's body. Like a disease it needs a cure.

At this point Moses announced that the nation of grumblers would wander the wilderness for forty years until that generation had died out (see Num 14). This was the cure for the disease. If the grumbling and self-centred people who had banded together against God's ways were not dealt with their poisonous attitude would have scuppered every new venture in the nation's future.

The Great Fire of London in 1666 was devastating to say the least but it destroyed any remnants of The Great Plague the year before. Perhaps it's time to set fire to grumbling in your life and let it burn until all remnants are gone.

Egypt is gone

So remember why you left Egypt. Improve your eyesight about what is in front of you. Put away that negative self-image because it is not how God sees you. Don't get swallowed up by fear of what you might lose if you step up to that new challenge. Instead consider what might be gained. Avoid the snare of regret and the damaging thought 'if only'. Run away from self-deception and grumbling. Whatever your Egypt was or is it represents a genuine stage you must pass through. Yet, we are challenged to move on from Egypt. It is not the end of the journey, it is the beginning. Remember that we leave Egypt to know and experience something better than what Egypt had in store for us.

Chapter 13

Red Lights and Green Lights

A work colleague was recently unsuccessful in applying for a different role within the organisation we both work for. I could empathise as I had a similar experience in my previous job when I tried for promotion. I made a comment to my work colleague that it was a case of coming up against red lights at the moment. What made me say this? My mind had drifted to picturing a big roundabout outside a nearby town and the road around it that has a lot of traffic lights to get through. Some days it feels like you've timed it just right when all the lights stay on green as you drive around without having to stop. Other times it's as though all the lights turn red as you approach them forcing you to stop. I have come to appreciate that life is a lot about timing:

There is a time for everything and a season for every activity under heaven...a time to embrace and a time to refrain, a time to search and a time to give up (Ecclesiastes 3v1, 5b, 6a).

For my colleague a red light was signalling that it wasn't the right time for a change of role. As for myself, when I didn't get the position I was after in the previous job it was also a red light telling me it wasn't the right time to move in that direction. My workmates at the time encouraged me that the company had done me a favour – they could see the leaders of the organisation would want their 'pound of flesh' from whoever got the job. With the benefit of hindsight I understand now that the promotion would've put undue pressure on family life and the timing wasn't right. As someone who prayerfully considers God's will in those situations, I believe God put that red light there. I have discovered that we experience red lights and green lights throughout life and also periods of waiting between them.

In the previous chapter we saw how the Israelites had to overcome a few hurdles to enter their Promised Land. For our purpose here, it could be said that the nation disregarded the 'green light' God had given them at first. During their time of deliberating it turned to red. God decreed that none of the grumblers would therefore enter the Land (see Number 14v23ff.) The people tried to carry on as if the situation hadn't changed:

We have sinned...we will go up to the place the Lord promised
(Numbers 14v40).

Their leader Moses warned them not to proceed in this presumption, that God was not with them and the result would be disastrous (v41-43). Nevertheless, in their presumption they ploughed ahead regardless (see v44). What happened? Disaster as predicted (see v45).

It results in disaster if we fail to stop at a red light and press on regardless. When that happens it's no good blaming God or anything else for the arrogance of our own presumption. Alarm bells need to ring when a red light appears in our path and we need to take the necessary steps like slowing down and coming to a halt. This gives us breathing space to see how the land lies and to recognise a new direction being given to us.

We can become extremely proficient at planning our route ahead and we don't like approaching a red light when it doesn't fit our plans. The Israelites had to learn that when they turned away from God's plan the alternative does not end well. They would not get passed the red light without incident. Although I appreciate that God allows me to think for myself, there have been occasions when I presumed to know what's better for me than God and this hasn't served me well. I have made some poor choices trying to force my way through (or around) red lights. The outcomes which followed have led me to conclude that our plans can come to nothing because some things just aren't meant to be:

Life is what happens to you when you're busy making other plans –
John Lennon

As a Christian it has gradually dawned on me that God is not driven by my own timetable for my life and a particular Bible passage has now become lodged in my memory banks:

In his heart a man plans his course, but the Lord determines his steps (Proverbs 16v9).

For those who trust God, 'He is The Traffic Light Controller'. We can plan where and when we want red lights and green lights along the road but it's God who determines whether or not we're approaching red or green.

Watch the road

When I'm driving my car, I'm conscious that the situation on the road in front of me can change in a split second so it's important not to become distracted. If a set of traffic lights coming up are showing green it's still advisable that I slow down and keep paying attention; the lights might be green when I'm a close distance away but can change to red by the time I've arrived at them. If I'm not looking at this stage because I've presumed they would still be on green and allow me to keep going then I'm in for a shock; I'm either going to have to screech to a sudden halt or 'run the red light' and risk collision with another vehicle coming through the other way on green.

Balaam was a person in the Bible not paying attention properly to what was happening in the road ahead of him and had to be jolted suddenly because he was in danger of running a red light. The King of Moab wanted Balaam to put a curse on Israel when they entered his territory:

Balaam...went with the princes of Moab. But God was very angry when he went and the angel of the Lord stood in the road to oppose him (Numbers 22v21-22).

Balaam got caught in the moment and allowed himself to be pushed in a direction that wasn't right for him. Instead of recognising what was happening he pressed ahead as if he was wearing a blindfold. Balaam's donkey (that he rode on) wasn't wearing a blindfold and saw the red light of the angel in the road and turned off into a field (see Numbers 22v23). Balaam beat the donkey to get it back on the road. A similar scenario played out further along the road and then again a third time. Eventually, Balaam saw the red light (the angel blocking the way) and came to an abrupt halt (v31). He offers the excuse that he didn't realise what the problem was (v34) but at least once he is aware he is prepared to change direction (v34).

Most of the time there is plenty of warning that traffic lights are ahead and you would need to be blindfolded not to see them. This is plenty of opportunity to apply the brakes and not just allow the car's momentum to drive you along as if you have no control. It's up to all of us not just to be swept along with what's happening around us. Of course we make mistakes. Like Balaam we sometimes need the blindfold removing and to be confronted with that red light in the road. The good news for those who seek God's will to be done in their lives is that the God of the Bible is full of grace and patience. He throws up signs and opportunities on the approach so that we apply the brakes and learn to work with Him for a better way forward.

Listen to the Navigator

Although I've had plenty of experience driving without anyone else in the car it can be helpful to have someone alongside in the front passenger's seat to help navigate an unfamiliar road. We are not expected to navigate life's road with its many twists and turns on our own. Before leaving his followers Jesus reassured them they would be given a navigator:

And I will ask the Father, and he will give you another Counsellor to be with you forever – the Spirit of Truth. The world cannot accept him nor knows him. But you know him, for he lives with you and will be in you. I will not leave you as orphans (John 14v16-18a).

This Counsellor, The Spirit of Truth is identified as The Holy Spirit who will teach God's people all things (see John 14v26) and guide them into all truth (John 16v13). The apostle Paul who conducted missionary journeys (see book of Acts) which helped spread Christianity across most of the then known world was open to The Navigator (The Holy Spirit) guiding him and his companions through various stages of these journeys. At one point they thought they had a green light to enter Bithynia (Roman province in what is now modern day Turkey) but the record states the Spirit of Jesus (The Holy Spirit) would not allow them to (see Acts 16v12). The group came right to the border of the area before a red light from The Navigator (HS) guided them to bypass it.

There are times when we travel right to the border of going in the wrong direction. God can allow this to happen before He steps in and steers us another way via the prompting of His Holy Spirit. God is not in the habit of stopping us in our tracks at the last minute just for the fun of it. He provides us with many opportunities to take the best course but sometimes He will step in to keep us on track:

Paul and his companions travelled throughout the region of Phrygia (in southwest modern day Turkey) *having been* <u>*kept*</u> *by the Holy Spirit from preaching ...in...Asia* (Acts 16v6 –omissions and emphasis by this author).

The word 'kept' used in the New International Version is significant. This suggests The HS was doing more than simply blocking the way to Asia. The 'Navigator' was doing His job of guarding the people of God from an unhelpful path/agenda.

When there's a passenger in my car helping to navigate or as is often the case today a SATNAV system I can either be guided by the suggestions given or simply ignore them. It's not easy I know to bend to other ideas or ways of doing things when we are going full steam ahead. It means changing our mind and admitting we may have got it wrong. It will serve us well if we are humble enough to change like this and are prepared to bend to the influence of The Navigator.

Red Lights eventually turn to green

At the entrance to the building where I work there is a door which is opened using an electronic key (known as a fob). When I hold the fob over the keypad the red light turns to green very quickly but sometimes I've still managed to be too quick before red turns to green and had to try again. I remind myself now to wait for that green light before trying to open the door.

We live in an instant society with the Internet making information available at the press of a button. Communications like email, text and social networking sites result in a very fast flow of information and so we've become accustomed to not waiting long to get things done. It has been a contributing factor to the creation of an impatient society in which we now live. Waiting is a dying art.

We have talked a lot about red lights in this chapter. Consider also that red lights eventually turn to green. Although we must stop at a red light, this doesn't mean an indefinite wait. When we come to red lights in our circumstances we need to use that waiting opportunity to prepare and be ready to move when it changes to green, which it will at some point. No time spent in preparation is ever wasted and life is a lot about preparation. We study for years to prepare for the career we want; athletes train hard every day for years as preparation to fulfil their sporting dreams; Jesus spent thirty years preparing for three and a half years of ministry. To sum up what we're talking about here in three words: *Preparation, preparation, preparation.* Do you get what I mean?

What happens during the time of waiting and preparation between red lights and green lights? Giants are dealt with, eyes are opened and we develop perspective. When Israel's southern kingdom of Judah was overthrown and the people exiled to Babylon it wasn't going to be an instant return. The prophet Jeremiah proclaimed to the people that they would be subject to the Babylonian king for seventy years. This time would require them to turn their hearts back to God and reject the evil that led to their downfall. When the seventy years were complete they would be brought back to their homeland (see Jeremiah 29).

Learning to listen

Waiting for red lights to turn green is an opportunity for listening. By this I mean listening to what those issues confronting us are trying to tell us and dealing with it. When the Philistine warrior giant Goliath confronted the army of Israel and filled its ranks with fear the Goliath issue needed resolving before the rest of the Philistine army could be defeated. The answer came in the form of a boy named David. He had the right attitude to confront Goliath and the giant was defeated. He would've felt obvious fear but didn't let fear stop him doing what needed to be done. The red light of Goliath was the opportunity for faith to arise and character to be strengthened.

If we only ever run up against green lights we do not become good listeners in our own lives and giants will continue to haunt us. Red lights provide vital space to practice the art of listening.

When Paul and his companions were *kept* from preaching in Asia and from entering Bithynia they experienced a period of waiting through the night. During this time, Paul listened and was given a green light signal for Macedonia (northern Greece). He consulted with the rest of the group and all concluded it required a positive response: They headed for Macedonia immediately (see Acts 16v9-10).

Are you ready?

When the light turns green that tells us the season of waiting is ended. If I'm stopped at traffic lights on red it is likely I will be in a line of waiting traffic by the time they turn green. So when the lights go green it's no time to hang around. Once the green light came on for Macedonia Paul and his companions didn't stand about deliberating, waiting for further instructions. The red light had been clear, now the green light was equally clear and they drew the right conclusion. They had maximised the moment for waiting and were now ready when red turned to green. Let us maximise those moments to wait at the red lights in our daily journey and get ready to go when red eventually turns to green?

Chapter 14

The Process of Perseverance

Although we have looked at various principles in this rough guide to pressing on, it could be said that all of them point to one word: perseverance. I know from my own experience as a Christian that it's tempting to draw out formulas from the Bible which can be seen as the secrets of pressing on successfully. This of course springs from our continuous pursuit of quick fix solutions or shortcuts. The writer to the Hebrews has a different approach:

You need to persevere (Heb 10v36a)

The apostle Paul in writing to the church at Corinth compares faith in Christ to running a race. He urges them to *run in such a way as to get the prize* and reminds them that *everyone who competes in the games goes into strict training* (1 Cor 9v24b-25). British audiences will remember well the London 2012 Olympic Games where the home nation won 65 medals, 29 of them gold. Some of these successes came after years of setbacks and disappointments. A couple of Games before that I recall Kelly Holmes speaking after winning double gold in Athens 2004; she talked of it being the culmination of a 20 year journey overcoming injury problems and many other difficulties along the way. In other words, a few minutes of running resulting in being crowned Olympic champion followed 20 years of perseverance. The event of winning the prize came after a process. Often we seek the event without the process. Unlike the crown of Olympic glory the Christian believes in everlasting salvation through Jesus Christ; a crown which lasts beyond this life and into eternity (see 1 Cor 9v25). Yet, just like the Olympic athlete, the discipline of strict training is called for. The Bible tells us God disciplines those He loves (see Heb ch12). We disqualify ourselves for the prize if we look for a quick method of pressing on instead of the discipline and strict training that goes with the process of perseverance.

This all sounds very daunting (I hear you say) and we can take one glance at the challenging road ahead and instantly begin looking for the exit door. To help us here we need to slow the pace down and just lay hold of what is achievable for us one step at a time.

Try a little patience

In the past few months my old car has been in a garage more than once being worked on by mechanics at considerable expense to keep it roadworthy. Despite this it broke down the other day and it looks like it isn't going to be a quick fix repair job. I live in a rural area not famed for good public transport links and to own a car is not a luxury. My family will be impatient for a quick resolution. This is one of those many occasions which call for a little patience – a good place to start in the process of perseverance and an achievable one. The problems we face may be small ones to fix or big ones. Some problems can seem prolonged. We need to persevere by having a little patience. I dare us to try a little patience.

As a father of four children I understand that one of the words they don't want to hear from an early age (apart from 'no') is 'wait'. For example, the child typically approaches parent and asks 'can you get me a drink' (more of a demand than a question). The unwanted response from parent will be something like, 'yes, just give me a minute'. From the moment we are born, we have a natural inclination towards wanting things now. Patience is a virtue we are told but seems the least natural one to most people. When we do try showing a little patience, we find it's no easy road. Indeed, it's easier to continue on a path that isn't working particularly well rather than face the upheaval of a new situation requiring a little patience to settle into. I persisted in shaving with cheap razor blades for years even though it wasn't agreeing particularly well with my sensitive skin. I thought about changing to an electric razor but didn't want to go through several weeks of rough shaving as my skin adjusted to the change. Eventually I decided to try it and yes I did find it rough shaving for a couple of months until my skin adapted but now I'm getting good results and I'm glad I decided to make the adjustment. All it required was a little patience on my part. Patience can lead us through rough periods where we must learn to adjust.

Someone I used to work with recently moved away from the area to begin another job opportunity. This new situation proved difficult to settle into. I sent a message of encouragement to give it time to adjust properly. An adequate amount of time to settle and to adjust properly is crucial. During this time we are taken through a process that requires patience. Patience is a process not an event in that we don't suddenly get patience. The process is something that goes on within us and so we need to give ourselves time to grow in patience.

The Bible advises believers in Christ to clothe themselves with various qualities, patience being among them (see Colossians 3v12). I might not feel like putting on various items of clothing but it is advisable if the weather outside demands it. In order to persevere through circumstances we encounter which may prove very demanding on both out external and internal resources we do well to put on a layer (or two) of patience.

That decent bloke in the Bible named Job was given a whole lot of undeserved trouble and needed patience for what he endured. He lost his wealth, possessions, children and his own health as well. More than a little patience required here you might say. Whilst things eventually improved for him, Job had to patiently endure whilst God appeared to remain silent. The reader sees Job lose everything in chapters 1-2 and we wait until chapter 38 before God speaks. Job endured the test of the silence of God. He was conscious of something going on (even if he didn't know what it was). He had numerous 'comforters' but their advice didn't help. You may not understand the process you are going through right now and your situation may attract unhelpful comforters. The advice here is simply to go through the process, allow it to unfold. Through the process we become who and what we are purposed to be.

Paul advised the church to *be patient in trouble* (Romans 12v12 New Living Translation). Peter gave instruction that *it's commendable...to bear...unjust suffering* due to being *conscious of God* (1 Peter 2v19). Trouble can be endured patiently if we see it as part of a meaningful process. The Christian can be conscious of God's involvement with the process and that He is working a process within them of becoming more dependent on Him. This calls for a little patience. If the whole patience thing feels completely beyond our grasp never forget that a little patience can take us a long way and is a key step in the process of perseverance.

Hold fast

We do not want you to become lazy, but to imitate those who through faith and patience inherit what has been promised (Hebrews 6v12).

We can become lazy if we do not have motivation to keep pressing on. The motivation to patiently persevere and to keep moving forward is found in what is confidently expected at the end of the process. Those who entrust their lives to God are encouraged to stay focused on His faithfulness to keep His promises:

Let us hold unswervingly to the hope we profess, for he who promised is faithful (Heb 10v23).

To hold fast without wavering when the ship of our lives is tossed and turned by stormy seas, we need conviction based on assurances that have been given and can be relied upon. If we are racked with doubts then any effort to hold fast will be half-hearted at best. If, on the other hand, we are fully convinced of something then our contribution is wholehearted and nothing will be able to move us:

Therefore, my dear brothers, stand firm. Let nothing move you. Always give yourselves fully to the work of the Lord, because you know that your labour in the Lord is not in vain (1 Corinthians 15v58).

One of the Israelites who left Egyptian slavery for The Promised Land stood out among his contemporaries for his wholehearted approach. His name was Caleb. He tried to rally the people to believe the promises of God as they arrived at the threshold of Canaan. He stood firm as others melted with fear. The doubters ended up dying in the wilderness but Caleb held fast to the promises of God. He patiently persevered for decades in the wilderness and lived long enough to reap the rewards of his unswerving commitment (see Joshua 14v13-14).

We can't avoid stormy waters in this life but we can decide not to jump ship and to stay the course with conviction that something better awaits us at journey's end.

Hope against hope

To be patient, to hold fast, often means to hope against hope. By this I mean continuing in hope when all hope seems lost. Prisoners on America's Death Row continue to hope in a reprieve. People shipwrecked or taken hostage cling to the hope of being rescued when the odds are stacked against it. A Biblical example of the hopers against hope club is Abraham, held up for Christians as the 'Father of faith' (see Romans 4).

Abraham was told that his wife Sarah would have a child and that through this Abraham would be the father of many nations.

Abraham against all hope *faced the fact that his body was as good as dead – since he was about a hundred years old – and that Sarah's womb was also dead. Yet he did not waver through unbelief regarding the promise of God, but was strengthened in his faith and gave glory to God, being fully persuaded that God had power to do what He had promised* (Romans 4v18-21).

The words above which have just been read may seem like a fairytale to those who do not share the beliefs of the Christian Faith. In truth, stranger things have happened on this earth; people have fallen thousands of feet from aeroplanes without a parachute and survived; others have recovered from life-threatening illnesses/injuries when the odds were against it. The point not to miss here though is that Abraham's hope was not in his circumstances. His confidence that the promise would be fulfilled did not get thrown away in the face of seemingly overwhelming obstacles. He had momentum to persevere and to keep pressing on because he continued to hope against hope.

Visualisation

Hoping against hope requires a kind of tunnel vision where we visualise the end result and have a game plan to get there. Recently I read about a top sportsman talking about his game plan on the eve of a championship final. He spoke of his calmness and how he was visualising the type of game he was going to play in order to win. He did go on to win. Visualising the path ahead is necessary so that we persevere when hurdles need to be overcome.

Popular programmes shown on TV these days include those which help make homes more attractive for potential buyers and those which help shops or businesses to draw in more customers. In each case the so-called 'experts' offering advice and support have a clear picture of what they want to achieve and how this needs to be done.

All of us benefit from having a clear picture of where we are going and how we are going to get there. Otherwise, it will be more difficult to keep going and to arrive at our destination.

The apostle Paul kept visualising the prize of his heavenly reward for Christian service:

Forgetting what is behind and straining towards what is ahead, I press on towards the goal to win the prize for which God has called me heavenwards in Christ Jesus (Philippians 3v13b-14).

We can get past what threatens to hold us back and press through the pain towards what is ahead if we are clearly visualising a goal which is motivating us. Paul had a message for all Christians that their goal is higher than the things of this world where nothing lasts forever and he reminds them that ultimately their citizenship is in heaven (ref Philipp.3v20). So, suffering does not last forever – it is temporary and is achieving for them *an eternal glory that far outweighs them all* (see 2 Cor 4v17). Paul urges us to *fix our eyes* on this (see 2 Cor 4v18). The message is: Visualise, get tunnel vision and get fixated in the right way! The alternative means you will not last the course.

Whatever vision in life becomes our driving force it takes more than willpower or self-effort to see it fulfilled. These can have a part to play but something not of ourselves needs to be relied upon. The athelete must heed the advice from the coaching team. The struggling business must accept an offer of help if it is to survive. For the Christian every day brings fresh awareness of the need for God-reliance rather than self-reliance to see them through:

I can do everything through him who gives me strength (Philipp 4v13).

Those who rely on God's strength through their faith in Christ are positioned to rely on God's strength in the face of their own weakness. Paul wants the church to visualise God saying: *My power works best in your weakness* (ref 2 Cor 12v9 New Living Translation). This will help them to stay focused on finishing the race and winning their reward in heaven.

There are obviously many times when we feel inadequate for what lies ahead; the mountains to climb and the rough terrain to negotiate. We all need help for the journey. Keep visualising the rewards of getting to the finish line and lean on all help to get there. Whether it meets with your tastes or not the Bible encourages us to get fixated on Jesus for this purpose:

Let us run with perseverance the race marked out for us. Let us fix our eyes on Jesus, the author and perfector of our faith, who for the joy set before him endured the cross, scorning its shame and sat down at the right hand of the throne of God. Consider him who endured such opposition from sinful men, so that you will not grow weary and lose heart (Heb 12v1-3).

Jesus represented God in the flesh enduring unimaginable suffering whilst on earth, yet he was helped by keeping before him the vision of future reward. His servant Paul also knew tremendous hardship and catalogues some of these for us to ponder and hopefully be inspired by:

Five times I received from the Jews the forty lashes minus one. Three times I was beaten with rods, once I was stoned, three times I was shipwrecked, I spent a night and a day in the open sea, I have been constantly on the move. I have been in danger from rivers, in danger from bandits, in danger from my own countrymen, in danger from Gentiles (non Jews), *in danger in the city, in danger in the country, in danger at sea; and in danger from false brothers* (those falsely claiming to be Christians). *I have laboured and toiled and have often gone without sleep; I have known hunger and thirst and have often gone without food; I have been cold and naked. Besides everything else, I face daily the pressure of my concern for all the churches* (2 Cor 11v24-28, clarifications in brackets author's).

From this we may see it is an understatement to say that Paul suffered. However, his faith in Christ stood the test and he was enabled by God to persevere. He kept his eyes fixed ahead and he finished the race strong in God. His parting remarks to his apprentice Timothy put the hardship he endured into perspective:

As for me, my life has already been poured out as an offering to God. The time of my death is near. I have fought (the) *good fight, I have finished the race and I have remained faithful. And now the prize awaits me – the crown of righteousness that the Lord, the righteous Judge, will give me on that great day of His return. And the prize is not just for me but for all who eagerly look forward to his glorious return* (2 Tim 4v6-8 New Living translation except for definite article in brackets taken from New International Version).

Is your life filled with purpose? Do you have a vision that something better awaits? Perhaps you are just trudging along with little or no understanding of what life is all about. We all need a reason to carry on and we need a life that is focused on completion.

The Task at hand

Someone once said that 'if you want people to feel involved give them something to do.' I work with some people who need to be given a task otherwise they are like a ship without a rudder that drifts off course or an explorer without a compass who doesn't know where they are or which way to proceed. Making sense of where we are in life and which direction to take is guided very much by whether or not we have been assigned a purposeful task:

I consider my life worth nothing to me, if only I may finish the race and complete the task the Lord Jesus has given me – the task of testifying to the gospel of God's grace (Acts 20v24).

We can fill our lives with lots of tasks but the question to ask is: What is THE overriding task of my life? This author clearly believes the answer is found in Jesus Christ and makes no apology for such a bold statement. Jesus was clear about HIS overriding task:

He went around doing good and healing all who were under the power of the devil, because God was with him (Acts 10v38);

The reason the son of God appeared was to destroy the devil's work
(1 John 3v8b) – the devil's work was holding the power of sin and
death over people's lives.

Through the sacrificial death of his perfect life on the cross Jesus
paid the ransom for human sin, disarming the devil and destroying
his power forever (see Heb2v14). This is why the eye witness
testimony records his final words on that cross: IT IS FINISHED (Jn
19v30). As he moved towards this we are given insight to how he
saw the task at hand:

As the time approached for him to be taken up to heaven, Jesus
resolutely set out for Jerusalem (Luke 9v51).

Jesus stayed resolute even as he knew the suffering and death that
awaited him in Jerusalem. Turning back was not an option; his mind
was set. He got the job done and the words 'it is finished' sum this
up. According to the biblical record which testifies to the resurrection
of Jesus witnessed by hundreds of eyewitnesses (and more) Jesus
tasked his followers before leaving them with going into the world
and telling the good news about him (ref Matthew 28v19-20, known
as The Great Commission). This is the overriding task for the
believer in Jesus Christ. It becomes the passion which energises
their lives. We can fill our lives with many things. Jesus gave one
overriding task which fills an entire life and this is better by far. We
can persevere, we can keep pressing on as we look to Jesus who
didn't know how to fail; who focused on completion and who
resolutely declares over the lives of all who put their faith in him: IT
IS FINISHED.

Conclusion

You may be struggling to see the finish line at present and that can depend on circumstances: athletes running the 100m sprint arrive at the finish line very quickly compared to those doing the marathon. This work has sought to encourage us that we can reach the finish line but with the advice that self-reliance only takes us so far. In our homes we constantly move furniture around but if we're honest never quite get it just the way we want. Similarly, we move around the metaphorical 'furniture' in our lives all the time without really being totally satisfied. Here you have been presented with examples of how God watches over our lives, sees what we're dealing with and offers to rearrange the furniture in a way that leaves us more than satisfied with the results. Often, God guides us to throw out certain items of furniture which are old and worn and are no longer serving any worthwhile purpose.

Putting God in charge of clearing out the old and providing space for the new requires we relinquish self-control and take up His offer of help. This work has sought to give us reason to do just that. It means slowing down long enough to take stock of where we are heading. It has been the author's desire here to provoke a response in the reader, a challenge if you like, to cease being a spectator in your own life and recognise intervention may be urgently needed. The intervention if allowed will call for a little patience as change takes shape but the benefits will prove to be lasting.

So wrestle and overcome that fear of change. Talk to yourself (when no one is looking of course). Let go of those excuses holding you back and take that leap of faith. Visualise where you want to be and remain determined to get there. This author has been strengthened in various circumstances by his faith in Jesus Christ and has sought to provide an abundance of evidence for that here. The overriding desire in producing this record is to see us realise our potential and receive inspiration to keep pressing on to the finish line.

Printed in Great Britain
by Amazon.co.uk, Ltd.,
Marston Gate.